HERSTORY 2

The Legal History of Chinese American Women

美國華人女性法律史

By **Chang C. Chen, PhD, JD** 邱龍

ISBN : 9798714244360

LCCN : 1243280861

HERSTORY 2

The Legal History of Chinese American Women

Chang C. Chen, PhD, JD

Includes bibliographical references.

Foreword

Although the Chinese Exclusion Act was repealed in 1943, and the Civil Rights Act was passed in 1964, discrimination against Chinese Americans persists. Chinese women are often more vulnerable to the racial and gender discrimination than Chinese men.

During the last 5 years, Dr. Chiu* has spoken out against racial and gender discrimination in her first book, "Herstory: The Legal History of Chinese American Women" and accompanying exhibitions.

Dr. Chiu was born in Kaohsiung, Taiwan before becoming a US citizen. She earned her Ph.D and JD degrees in biochemistry and law from Columbia University, and went on to practice law for 35 years. She noticed that it was often Chinese women, not men, who persisted in using the rule of law to stand up for themselves. At times, this stance even resulted in abandonment and betrayal by their family and friends, as they challenged the status quo. Through these legal cases, these courageous women made their mark on the legal history of the United States, a nation rooted in the rule of law.

After a decade of travelling back and forth between the U.S., Taiwan and Hong Kong without funding support, Dr. Chiu has researched and collected undiscovered cases involving Chinese American women. Digging through piles of dusty documents from the US Supreme Court and the California Supreme Court, she has invested time and resources in uncovering the human stories hiding behind the legalese.

In 2012 Dr. Chiu published "The Battle Between the Dragon and the Eagle: Legal History of Chinese Americans," which records how those women fought for their rights with resilience and perseverance through the American legal system.

At the end of 2014, Dr. Chiu came to visit me at the National History Museum of Taiwan. I learned that although we had never met, we actually studied in the same building at the National Taiwan University from 1968 to 1972. Dr. Chiu studied Botany while I was a Zoology major. After graduation, she became a lawyer, and I became the

*Dr. Chiu is Dr. Chang C. Chen's maiden name

director of the National History Museum. I did not expect that I would meet her in the Museum 40 years later.

Dr. Chiu told me that she wanted to curate an exhibition based on the struggles and success stories of Chinese American women. Using a combination of art and multimedia, she hoped to share these stories in a more visual way than one could experience by reading a book.

At the time, I had been the director of the Museum for nearly five years and I was thinking about changing the exhibitions to better resonate with public sentiment. Therefore, when Dr. Chiu proposed this exhibition, I was so excited that I immediately agreed.

In June 2015, the exhibition of "Herstory: Chinese American Women, 165 Years of Struggle and Success" opened to the public on the fourth floor of the National History Museum of Taiwan. In addition to the historical documents and pictures of the lawsuits brought by Chinese American women from 1874 to 2012, Dr. Chiu also invited a group of master artists, such as Chen Chieh-Jen and Yuan Guangming to exhibit large-scale epic sketches, videos and other multimedia installations for the Chinese American Women in Herstory.

The highlight of the exhibition was a "Mirror Palace" in the center of the exhibition hall where Taiwan Glass Team used 52 large mirrors to reflect precious historical photos etched in glass plates shining above the ground covered with glass sand. The audience was filled with awe when they were confronted by the reflection of the historical figures while listening to their stories. This exhibition with its unique theme and special display techniques was truly amazing. Many visitors expressed their gratitude to the National History Museum and requested more similar exhibitions in the future.

In conjunction with this exhibition, Dr. Chiu also published the book, "Herstory" She was determined to extend the influence of Herstory to the United States.

Through her efforts, the Herstory exhibition travelled to 22 major U.S. public libraries from 2016 to 2019, including San Francisco, Berkeley, Los Angeles, San Diego, Chicago, New York, and Hawaii. The exhibition had been kept in the New York Public Library, Chatham Square Branch for an unprecedented 2.5 years. Dr. Chiu was very happy to learn that Chinese American women, as a new social identity, had finally been recognized.

Dr. Chiu recently told me she wanted to continue to write and exhibit "Herstory 2",

and she asked me to write a foreword for this book. "Herstory 2" consists of two parts. The first part describes legal cases where Chinese American women fought for justice. The second part describes Chinese American women involved in politics. I read her manuscript with great interest. I am embarrassed to admit that out of the 27 women in her book, I had only heard of less than half.

Through Dr. Chiu's painstaking research and heart-wrenching writing, the faces and lives of these women were brought to life and I was deeply moved. I thank Dr. Chiu for giving me the opportunity to read her manuscript, and I am sure readers will be inspired by this book as well.

Five years ago, if you had searched in the index of the Library of Congress for the phrase "Chinese American Women", you would not have found a single result. Now, thanks to Dr. Chiu's effort, you will find more than 300,000 entries. Chinese American women have finally secured their place in American history.

張譽騰

前國立歷史博物館館長 / 前中華民國博物館學會理事長

Dr. Chang Yu-tung

Former General Director of the National Museum of History, Taiwan

Former Chairman of the National Association of Museums, Taiwan

留取丹心照汗青：
邱彰再接再厲為美國華人女性寫史

今年 (2020 年) 5 月 25 日美國明尼蘇達州的明尼亞波利斯市黑人男子弗洛依德（George Floyd）在被白人警察逮捕過程中，因為壓頸導致死亡，引起全美大規模示威抗議，「黑命珍貴」（Black Lives Matter）口號成為輿論焦點。美國社會的民權狀況雖然因為 1964 年通過的《民權法案》迭有改善，但對有色人種的歧視與排斥仍然時有所聞。

以美國華人為例，「排華法案」早在 1943 年廢除，華人在美國社會依然是弱勢團體，甚至比黑人還不如。在華人群體中，女性更是弱勢中的弱勢，經常籠罩在歧視與排斥陰影之下。

令人欣慰的是，總有人願意站出來，為在陰影中的華人女性爭取尊嚴和權利、伸張正義，邱彰律師就是這個代表。過去十年來，她念茲在茲，持續為華人女性發聲，以美國華人女性奮鬥史為主題，陸續出版書籍和策劃展覽，把華人女性被忽略的歷史一一展現在世人面前。

邱彰出生於台灣高雄，畢業於北一女和台大，取得哥倫比亞大學生物化學博士及法學博士後入籍美國，擔任律師已近三十五年，親身經歷多樁華人訴訟案。她發現在這些訴訟中，不屈不撓、堅持打官司的往往不是男性，而是女性。這些女性不惜違背華人「訟終凶」的祖訓，勇敢的為自己、為孩子、為家庭爭取平權，甚至在遭遇丈夫、家人背叛拋棄的情況下，依然堅持不懈。通過種種訴訟，她們在美國這個法治大國裡，寫下了令人動容的法律故事，創造出嶄新的華人歷史。

過去十年來，無任何經費支持下，邱彰在美國、台灣、香港等地穿梭奔走，蒐集、鑽研、爬梳罕為人知的美國華人法律事件，特別著墨於華人女性的鋪陳。

在無數個挑燈夜戰日子裡，她埋首於美國最高法院及加州最高法院塵封多年資料，釐清出眾多僵硬法律用語背後這些血淚交織的故事。

2012 年，邱彰出版了《龍與鷹的搏鬥：美國華人法律史》，這是一本記載美國華人上法庭爭取權利的書。在這本有血有肉的書裡，記載了許多華人女性自十九世紀被賣至美國為奴迄今，在異域裡爭取人權的艱苦過程。同為華人女性，又在美國創業，邱彰特別能夠切身體會這些華人女性在美國社會奮鬥的遭遇。書裡細述了她們如何從開始完全被排斥，備受歧視和屈辱，卻能發揮女性特有韌性，終於出人頭地的歷程。

2014 年年底，邱彰律師到國立歷史博物館找我，一聊之下，才知道我倆雖素未謀面，其實在台大同一棟樓一起學習了四年，當年她讀台大植物系，我讀台大動物系，系館都在一號館。畢業後她成為律師，我也轉行成為國立歷史博物館館長，沒想到四十年後竟然在博物館碰頭。

邱彰告訴我，她想辦一個以華人女性奮鬥史為主題的展覽，通過展覽，可以運用藝術和多媒體方式，把事實傳達給觀眾，會比書籍直接也更容易進入人們的視線。為此，她用了三年時間四處奔走，搜集展覽素材，希望能詳盡地把華人女性被忽略的歷史展現世人面前。

當時我任館長已近五年，覺得國立歷史博物館不應該老是辦畫展，應該要重新思考定位和轉型問題；亦即博物館應該如何和社會脈動共振，讓歷史以當代民眾關心的形式呈現出來。因此，當邱彰提出這個展覽建議時，我怦然心動，當下就答應了。

2015 年 6 月，《她的故事—華人女性 165 年的奮鬥史》(Herstory: Chinese American Women 165 Years of Struggle and Success) 在國立歷史博物館四樓與社會大眾見面。除了提供 1847 年至 2012 年間美國華人女性法律訴訟史的文獻圖片之外，邱彰並邀請到一群大師級藝術家如陳界仁、袁廣鳴等義助展出，以大幅史詩素描、錄像製作、環繞投影等多媒體裝置，再現這些華人女性在美國法律事件中的身影。最大亮點是台灣玻璃團隊在展場中心建造一座由五十二片大鏡子組成的「鏡子宮殿」，一系列歷史珍貴照片被轉印在玻璃上面，地上鋪滿玻璃細沙映照著觀眾，讓他們在歷史長流裡跟這些華人女性邂逅，聽她們訴說一段段動人心弦的故事。

配合這個展覽，邱彰同時出版了《她的故事》(Herstory) 這本書。這個展覽由於主題鮮明，展示手法特別，引起許多迴響。有些觀眾還特別來電，認為這才是國立歷史博物館的正業，建議爾後應該多舉辦這樣的展覽。

《她的故事─華人女性 165 年的奮鬥史》的台灣展出非常成功，但邱彰並不滿足於此。她決心要繼續把展覽帶到美國本土，將這段歷史呈現給美國當地民眾，讓他們了解華人女性群體在美國土地上是如何為平權而戰。

邱彰積極與美國各州州立、市立圖書館和大學圖書館溝通，一步一腳印，從 2016 年開始到 2019 年，這個展覽陸續在舊金山、柏克萊、洛杉磯、聖地牙哥、芝加哥、紐約和夏威夷等地的 22 家州立或大學圖書館展出，在美國最大的紐約圖書館展出時間場長達史無前例的 2.5 年之久。雖然有些美國觀眾並不能了解展覽的深層意涵，但是華人女性概念已經開始出現在他們腦海，留下印象，對於邱彰來說，這就是一件非常滿足的事情。

出版書籍或策畫展覽對邱彰來說，並沒有甚麼功利目的，如果有的話，僅僅是想把這些華人女性歷史真相呈現給世界，希望有更多人知道。她有一個心願：希望年輕人能夠對這個題材感興趣，可以找到接班人，繼續播種、傳承自己多年心血。

最近，邱彰傳簡訊給我，說她想出版《她的故事續集》(Herstory II)，而且稿子已經寫好了，希望我寫序。全書分成兩部分，第一部分標題是「華人女性在美國為爭取正義奮鬥」，描寫 13 個華人女性在美國爭取尊嚴和權利的故事，

第二部分標題是「華人女性參政」，敘述 10 位在美國參政的傑出華人女性的事蹟。我仔細閱讀書稿，很慚愧的是，23 位美國華人女性當中，我聽過的還不到一半。透過邱彰的深入調查研究和撼動人心的手筆，這些女性的面貌和事蹟躍動在眼前，讓我久久難以釋懷。感謝邱彰讓我有機會先睹為快，相信本書出版後一定也會感動很多讀者。

五年前，如果有人到美國國會圖書館（Library of Congress）在線搜索系統查找「華裔女性」（Chinese American Woman）這個關鍵字，幾乎很難看到任何相關記錄。現在情況迥然不同，輸入這個關鍵字後，已經可以找到三十多萬條記錄，而且每天還不斷增加。這些記錄的意義重大，意味著華人女性歷史已經有了可追溯的根源，後人能夠根據這些記錄去「認識、了解和感謝」(to know, to understand and to appreciate) 這些華人女性的奮鬥歷程和動人成就。邱彰在這方面的努力和堅持值得我們敬禮。

A tribute to the perseverance of Chinese American Women

To me, Dr. Chiu Chang was an unapproachable celebrity. I could only see her on TV shows and the news. However, I was lucky enough to meet her when I led students from the Department of Library and Information Science of both Fu Jen Catholic University and Taiwan University to intern at the San Francisco Public Library. Dr. Chiu graciously provided her home to host my students and me during our stay. I was very impressed by her warmth and wisdom.

Before my trip to San Francisco, I picked up one of Dr. Chiu's books, "The Battle Between the Dragon and the Eagle: Legal History of Chinese Americans." I wanted to get to know her better. Reading on long flights usually puts me to sleep right away, but this time I read the entire book and was moved to tears.

Although I pursued my graduate degree in the United States, I was unaware of the discrimination that Chinese women before me had to endure. I did not know how staunchly they fought for equal treatment under the law. Through Dr. Chiu's book, I began to understand that when my generation came to the U.S., we were fortunate enough to benefit from the progress made by those pioneers. It was because of their hard work and contributions that we did not have to face the same discriminatory environment.

In her book, Dr. Chiu told the story of Dr. Mi Chu, originally from Taiwan who eventually became the Asia specialist in the Asian Division of the Library of Congress. When she first applied for a position in 1977, despite her excellent qualifications, she was rejected even for an interview. She sued under the Equal Employment Opportunity Act and won. She worked for the Library of Congress for 35 years until she retired. Her success paved the way for many more Chinese American women seeking equal employment opportunities after her.

A Chinese proverb explains, "The first generation planted the trees so that the future generation can enjoy the shade." I believe Dr. Chiu is a "tree planter" because of her groundbreaking research in the field of the legal history of Chinese American women.

Dr. Chiu is highly motivated by this important mission. She continues to write inspiring stories of Chinese American women. Her most important book, HERSTORY: The Legal History of Chinese American Women was published in 2016; she also curated a travelling-exhibition of the same topic.

She and I remain friends after my visit, and she keeps me updated on her work documenting many trailblazing Chinese American women. I admire her for her effort. I think Dr. Chiu is writing herstory herself.

In her new book HERSTORY 2: The Legal History of Chinese American Women, she writes stories about congresswomen, physicians, police chiefs, judges, and many more while focusing on contemporary women. I believe after reading Herstory 2, you will be just as inspired and encouraged as I am.

黃元鶴
輔仁大學圖書資訊學系教授

Yuanhe Huang

Professor, Department of Library and Information Science, Fu Jen Catholic University

「堅忍剛毅、自強不息」向可歌可泣的美國華裔女性奮鬥史致敬

　　最初對邱彰博士的印象，僅是在電視或新聞報導上才會看到的知名人物，對我來說，可謂遙不可及。而後有幸得識邱博士，乃是藉由帶領輔仁大學與臺灣大學二校圖書資訊學系的學生到美國舊金山市立圖書館海外實習的機緣，由於當時邱博士慷慨地提供實習期間的免費住宿給學生們，於是我也得以隨同在邱博士家中叨擾了一週，建立了我對邱博士熱心公益及平易近人的深刻印象。

　　出發前為了能夠更加認識她，我便先在輔大圖書館的館藏目錄上檢索，得知其大作《龍與鷹的搏鬥：美國華人法律史》一書，借出後隨即放入行篋，打算在飛往舊金山的途中拜讀。依個人的經驗，通常在長途飛行的旅程裡，閱讀總會使我很快的進入夢鄉，但此書卻不同於以往，我在飛機上一口氣讀完後，竟然是不自覺地眼眶濕潤，心情激動，久久不能平復。

　　即便我曾經留學美國，但從來不知道在美國的女性華人曾經遭受如此不平等的對待，以及這些前輩們又是如何付出比一般人更多的努力來爭取平等。透過這本書，才讓我深刻體認到今日赴美的女性華人，不論求學或工作，之所以能夠不會感覺法律或體制的不友善，其實都應該感謝前輩們的披荊斬棘，為後人開創的康莊大道。

　　例如書中收錄的人物之一：前美國國會圖書館亞洲部學術研究主任居蜜博士，在邱博士的筆下即細膩地批露出她最初是如何受到就業歧視、後來又如何捍衛己身專業與權益，終於得以創下首位臺灣女性在美國通過《平等就業機會法》的案例，如今美國已有不少華裔女性圖書館員在各類型圖書館中安然就業。當然，最終還得歸功於邱博士總結相關史料，完成該書出版問世，才使我頓悟原來在美國求學時期的順利平安，必須心存感恩。俗謂：「前人種樹，後人乘涼」，既然透過邱博士的大作才使後人知道有哪些「種樹者」，因此在我的心

目中，邱博士當然也是「種樹者」之一。

　　邱博士具有強烈的民族使命感，她未以出版一本華裔女性法律史而滿足，她持續戮力爬梳具有影響力的美國華裔女性的奮鬥事蹟，詔告世人。除了在2016 年繼續出版《HERSTORY：The Legal History of Chinese American Women》一書外，亦曾策展同名的展覽，讓更多人知曉華裔女性的堅毅與自強不息。

　　時至今日，偶爾我仍會收到邱博士傳來的訊息，有時是她完稿某位華裔女性的故事，有時是她為某位華裔女性奮鬥過程製作的口述歷史書籍。我相當佩服邱博士，這麼多年來持續不斷地投入許多心力與資源於蒐集華裔女性奮鬥史資料，並加以推廣，在美國各地的圖書館或博物館巡迴展覽，讓更多的人能夠瞭解美國華裔女性的奮鬥歷程，藉以激勵人心。我深刻覺得，在她寫書與推廣大眾認識美國華裔女性的努力過程中，她自己本身也正在撰寫歷史，為往後的美國華人史研究留下深遠的影響力。

　　此刻邱彰博士又更加深邃的探究這個主題，發表新書《HERSTORY 2：The Legal History of Chinese American Women》，將研究對象拓展到各式各樣職業的華裔女性，包含餐廳經營者、州務卿、參議員、眾議員、醫師、警察局長、法官等，內容包括她們爭取女性投票權的始末、性侵案的受害人影響陳述……等，詳實探討許多轟轟烈烈的血淚故事，個案的時間點也從歷史走向當代，跨越不同世代的華裔女性，嘗試在各種不同層面，呈現她們不屈不撓的為平權奮鬥的故事，是一本看了會讓人心生憐憫、振奮人心的佳作。相信在閱讀這些「化悲憤為力量」的故事後，讀者必會受到相當程度的啟發與鼓勵，進而產生許多迎向未來、奮鬥不懈的正能量。

為 Herstory 喝采

　　我來美較早，1960 年就定居美國，所以對台灣的事務及名人，知之甚少，唯獨對台灣邱彰立法委員的大名及她的事蹟，卻是聞名久矣。

　　20 年前，我跟她在美國初遇，對她不屈不撓的精神及她對理想的執著，十分感動。當我知道她要把 165 年來中國女性在美國的辛酸史、奮鬥史一一挖掘出書，寫成傳記，在博物館展出或發行書籍，以供大眾了解，我舉雙手贊成。

　　無論古今社會、中外國家，對女性的歧視根深蒂固，西方倡導的男女平權，更像是男性在社會中唱的高調，所謂 Lady First 無非源自男性優越感的陶侃。重男輕女的概念讓一般人都認為人類歷史就是男人故事的記錄，而社會之所以形成及發展都歸功於男性的努力，至於歷史的延續也是男人奮鬥的結果，history 直白翻譯，就是「男人的故事」。

　　但邱彰博士卻深信女人照樣可以創造歷史，女人的奮鬥也是歷史的動力，女人的故事也是歷史過程中的一部分，所以邱彰把編著的美國華人女性法律史定名為 Herstory，此字直翻就是「女人的故事」，令我拍案叫絕。

　　2016 年她出版了第一本 Herstory「她的歷史」，2020 年出版了 Herstory 2。在第一本中，她寫出 1852 至 2012 年 35 個創造華人里程碑的案件，在第二本中，她寫出 1912 年至 2020 年 17 個重要的法律案例，還列出 2000 年至 2018 年 10 位華人女性政治人物。這兩本書彰顯了美國司法的優缺點，也明示華人女性在美國社會地位提昇的軌跡。

　　凡走過必留下痕跡，美國華人女性的法律史不該被埋沒，根據邱彰的記載，我希望所有過去及今天華人女性的努力，都會為我們下一代開創更好的未來。

　　歷史是人類生活的記錄，所以記錄中應該有他，也有她。

方李邦琴

報人，北京大學榮譽校董

Preface

The exhibition of "Herstory-The Legal History of Chinese American Women" first opened on June 18, 2015 in the National Museum of History in Taipei, Taiwan. As its curator, I was both excited and terrified, and I was very lucky to have a team of talented artists who supported me in planning, designing and composing the artwork. As a result, the exhibition attracted nearly 200,000 visitors in three months.

The exhibition included a spell-bounding mirror maze that was constructed from 52 huge mirrors and measured 9 feet in diameter. As soon as you walked into the mirror maze, you felt you were in heaven: stars shone brightly above and the stories of women illuminated on a floor of glass sand embedded with millions of tiny LED lights.

The Herstory exhibition and related book grew in popularity as it shed light on a previously undocumented piece of history: Chinese American women and their challenges to gain recognition, suffrage, respect and a voice. From the first exhibit in Taipei, Herstory's photo exhibition was invited to 22 major libraries across the United States. At the New York Public Library, the exhibition was held there for an unprecedented 2.5 years, until the library had to be renovated.

I also travelled to many U.S. cities including San Francisco, Los Angeles, Chicago, and even Honolulu for Herstory exhibitions. No matter where I went, I could feel the enthusiasm and the sincerity of people's support. I realized that women hold up half the sky.

By 2019, I had seen quite a few more stories that are undoubtedly part of the legal history of Chinese American women. These include the sexual discrimination lawsuit filed by Ellen Pao and the #MeToo Movement. I also saw more than ten Chinese American women elected to government office who became Senators, Assemblywomen and Mayors. Herstory was taking place in front of my eyes and I was inspired by these courageous individuals to write Herstory 2.

Many people thought that when women won the right to vote in 1920, full equality between men and women would be accomplished, but they were wrong. Women in America are only making progress toward equality step-by-step:

In 1938, federal law sets an equal minimum wage for both sexes.

In 1964, Congress outlaws job discrimination based on gender.

In 1965, states can no longer outlaw contraception in marriages.

In 1968, the year the term "Chinese American" was born.

In 1972, Title IX opens opportunities for female athletes in federal funded schools.

In 1973, Roe v. Wade was decided, the Supreme Court rules that a woman has the right to terminate a pregnancy.

In 1974, Dr. March Fong Eu became the first Chinese American female Secretary of State of California.

In 1974, Congress makes it illegal to deny credit cards based on sex or marital status.

In 1978, Congress bars employers from firing women for becoming pregnant.

In 1989, in Helen Liu v. Republic of China, 892 F.2d 1419, the court held that the Act of State doctrine does not mandate abstention in cases where a foreign government ordered the assassination of an American citizen in the United States.

In 2009, federal law Fair Pay Act makes it easier for victims of pay discrimination to file legal complaints.

In 2016, all military positions, including combat positions, become available to women.

In 2017, the #MeToo Movement was ignited when more than 53,000 tweets and 12 million Facebook posts call out sexual harassment.

In 2018, Chanel Miller, a Chinese American woman changed the laws on sexual assault.

In 2020, Kamala Harris becomes the first woman elected Vice President of the U.S.

The road is tortuous, but the future is bright. Chinese American women have not only weathered gender inequality, but racial discrimination as well. Herstory 2 documents the contributions they have made to earn their well-deserved place in history.

Chang C. Chen
2021

Preface

2015 年 6 月 18 日，我策展的「Herstory- 美國華人女性法律史」在台北國立歷史博物館開幕，這是我第一次作為策展人，真是又惶恐又興奮，還好我有一個超炫的藝術家團隊，共同策劃、設計及製成亮麗的展品，讓我們在短短三個月的展出期間，吸引了近 20 萬人參觀。

你一定會喜歡我們的鏡子宮殿！踏入這個直徑九公尺，由 52 片鏡子組成的神奇宮殿，你恍惚置身天堂，四周星光璀璨，一位又一位傑出的女性在時光的長河裡，低訴她們的故事。

Herstory 展覽巡迴到了美國，我們受到 22 家最大的圖書館邀約，包括紐約公共圖書館，Herstory 在紐約展出史無前例的兩年半，一直到該館必須維修為止。

我的足跡也走遍了舊金山、洛杉磯、芝加哥，還遠征夏威夷，無論我走到那裡，我都能感受到濃濃的熱情和真摯的支持，我意識到華人女性在美國真的是撐起了一片天。

展覽辦到 2019 年，期間發生了很多法律史的大事，包括 Ellen Pao 的驚天訴訟，還有讓全世界女性義憤填膺的 #MeToo 運動，我也看到了超過 10 位華人女性當選聯邦眾議員、各州參眾議員和市長，她們的出類拔萃，在這個文化大熔爐裏發出耀眼的光芒，我被她們感動及激勵，Herstory 2- 華人女性法律史第二部於焉出爐。

很多人以為美國女性在 1920 年得到了選舉權，男女平權就不是問題了，但在 1920 年之後持續發生的兩性平權之爭，說明了男女的同工同酬到今天都還只是個理想，女性還是必須一步一腳印的走下去，請看我們的足跡！

1920 年，美國女性獲得選舉權。

1938 年，聯邦制定兩性平等的「最低工資法」。

1964 年，國會認定在工作上的性別歧視是非法的。

1965 年，各州不得再禁止女性於婚後選擇避孕。

1972 年，教育法第 9 號修正案通過，禁止接受聯邦經費的教育機構有任何性別歧視行為。

1973 年，最高法院在 *Roe v. Wade* 明示女性有權終止自己的懷孕。

1974 年，余江月桂成為加州首位華人女州務卿。

　　國會認定因為性別或婚姻狀況，而拒絕信用卡的申請為非法。

1978 年，國會禁止雇主因為女性員工懷孕而將其解雇。

1981 年，Sandra Day O'Conner 成為第一位最高法院女性大法官。

1989 年，***崔蓉芝 訴 中華民國 892 F.2d 1419*** 一案，第九巡迴法院判定「國家行為原則」不能阻止法院聽證外國政府在美國本土刺殺美國公民的案件。

2009 年，聯邦「*公平支付法*」讓受薪資歧視的受害人較容易提起訴訟。

2016 年，所有的軍方職位包括第一線的作戰，女性都可以申請加入。

2017 年，全世界女性分享她們受性騷擾的經驗，點燃了 #MeToo 運動。

2018 年，張小夏重寫加州關於性侵的立法。

2020 年，賀錦麗成為美國第一位女性民選美國副總統。

　　道路是崎嶇的，前途是光明的，美國華人女性經歷了性別不平等與種族歧視，不屈不饒的寫下了輝煌的美國華人女性法律史，為自己在美國史上贏得重要的席位。

邱彰

2021 年 1 月 22 日於舊金山

目錄 | CONTENTS

美國華人女性法律史

華人女性的左一七八五年来美國在隨後的兩百多年裏她們在美國這個法治大國裡寫下了全人類罕見的法律故事

他們先是爭取成為美國公民的機會然後無懼的為自己爭取尊嚴我們將展出他們寫下的法律史HerStory以免他們的故事在史冊裡被埋沒透過這個展覽這群為我們鋪路的女性終於可以發聲了

HERSTORY 2

1912

Mabel Ping-Hua Lee fought for women's suffrage

On August 18, 1920, the 19th Amendment to the U.S. Constitution was ratified, granting American women the right to vote. The legislation, however, had very little effect on those outside the upper and middle-class white women at that time. Among those excluded was Mabel Ping-Hua Lee, who fought for women's suffrage.

Born on October 7, 1897, Lee was raised in Guangzhou, China. Her family emigrated to the U.S. in 1905. They reportedly settled in a tenement at 53 Bayard Street in New York City's Chinatown.

In 1912, at the age of sixteen, she helped lead a parade of 10,000 people advocating for women's suffrage while riding a white horse. In 1917, Lee received a master's degree from Barnard College and later became the first woman to receive a Ph.D. from Columbia University, along with a Boxer Indemnity Scholarship from the Chinese government.

In a 1914 issue of the Chinese Students' Monthly at Barnard, she wrote, "The welfare of China and possibly its very existence as an independent nation depends on rendering justice to its womankind. For no nation can ever make real and lasting progress in civilization unless its women are following close to its men if not actually abreast with them. "

Despite the ratification of the 19th Amendment in 1920, because of the Chinese Exclusion Act of 1882, which denied U.S. citizenship to Chinese immigrants, Lee herself remained unable to vote. It was not until 1943 when Chinese immigrants were finally granted American citizenship and the right to vote.

On December 3, 2018, the U.S. Postal Service dedicated Manhattan's Chinatown post office in Lee's honor, naming it the Mabel Lee Memorial Post Office. This designation was introduced through a bill by Congresswoman Nydia Velázquez, who said, "At a time when women were widely expected to spend a life in the home, Lee shattered one glass ceiling after another. From speaking out in the classroom to organizing Chinese American women to secure the right to vote, Lee's bold vision for Chinatown is very much alive in our community today. "

As a devout Baptist, she dedicated the rest of her life to the church and the Chinatown community until her death in 1966 at the age of 70.

MISS MABEL LEE, Secretary

Lee in the Chinese Student Monthly at
Barnard College (1915).

MABEL LEE
The young Chinese woman who wants a vote.

CHINESE GIRL WANTS VOTE

Miss Lee Ready to Enter Barnard, to Ride in Suffrage
Parade.

THIS BUILDING IS NAMED
IN HONOR OF

MABEL LEE

BY AN ACT OF CONGRESS
PUBLIC LAW
115-212
JULY 24, 2018

Mabel Lee Memorial Post Office

1912

李彬華爭取女性投票權

　　李彬華，1897 年出生於廣州， 1905 年隨母親移民至紐約與父親團聚，住在紐約中國城。1912 年，16 歲的她騎在白馬上，帶領了一萬名女性遊行，要求婦女也有選舉權。

　　1913 年，她進入巴納德學院，1914 年她在中國學生月刊裡寫到，"中國作為一個獨立國家的本質，就在於它是否能提供女性同胞遲來的正義。因為沒有任何國家可以在人類文明上做出真正長久的貢獻，除非它的女性能與男性並駕齊驅。"

　　1921 年，她成為哥倫比亞大學第一位獲得博士學位的女性。1920 年，美國憲法第 19 條修正案通過，禁止任何公民因為性別而被剝奪選舉權，美國婦女終於獲得選舉權，但李彬華卻因為當時的排華法案無法投票。1943 年，華人才獲得公民權及投票權。

　　2018 年 12 月 3 日，紐約中國城的郵局改名為"李彬華紀念郵局"，提出這個法案的眾議員 Nydia Velazquez 說， "在一個女性待在家裡做主婦的年代裡，李彬華打破了一個又一個的玻璃天花板。她從年輕時在教室裡的敢言不懼，到後來組織華人女性爭取選舉權，李彬華對中國城的願景，在今天我們的社區中依舊栩栩如生。"

　　李彬華是虔誠的基督教浸信會員，她生前全心全意為教會及社區服務，直到 1966 年過世，享年 70 歲。

1932

"Comfort Women": The Silenced Victims

"Comfort women" were young women forced into sex slavery in the Japanese occupied territories during World War II. As many as 400,000 young women came from Korea, China and South East Asia who were abducted from their homes and incarcerated in "comfort stations".

They were beaten and raped over 30-40 times each day, and forced to donate blood to wounded Japanese soldiers. Three quarters of them died during captivity.

Beginning in 1991, comfort women from China, Taiwan, Korea and the Philippines sued the Japanese government, demanding a formal apology and compensation. Although the Japanese government admitted wrongdoing, the Japanese courts threw out the cases, based on : "Individuals cannot sue the government" and that "the statute of limitation" had expired. To this day, most Japanese adults and students are ignorant of this tragedy.

In 2007, the U.S. House of Representatives passed House Resolution 121, urging the Japanese government to incorporate the actual historical facts about comfort women into their educational curriculum. But the Japanese government did not comply. Former Secretary of State Hilary Clinton was a strong advocate of the cause, and denounced the use of the euphemism "comfort women" for what should be referred to as "enforced sex slaves."

Starting in 2011, statutes of comfort women were erected all over the world. The statute depicts a young woman clutching her fist, angrily staring at the Japanese government's denial of its war crime towards women.

In 2013, a comfort women memorial statue, the Peace Monument of Glendale in Southern California was erected. In 2014, a Japanese government-backed plaintiff sued the City of Glendale to remove the statute arguing that the installation of the statue exceeds the power of the City, and infringes on the U.S. government's ability to handle foreign affairs. A federal judge dismissed the lawsuit. On appeal, Judge Kim McLane Wardlaw of the Ninth Circuit Court of Appeal opined, "To set up the statue, the City is taking a stand against human rights violation, it is well within the traditional responsibilities of state and local government." Gingery v. City of Glendale, No.14-56440 (9th Cir. 2016).

舊金山慰安婦雕像，在揭幕前。

1932

慰安婦 --- 被消音的受害者

　　慰安婦是二次世界大戰期間，在日本佔領的土地上，被日軍強迫做性奴的年輕女性。有將近 400,000 名韓國、中國及東南亞的女性從家中被綁架，囚在慰安所，每天被打及強暴超過 30-40 次，日軍受傷時還要捐血。她們之間有四分之三在被囚期間死亡。

　　1991 年中國、台灣、韓國的慰安婦向日本政府提告，要求正式道歉及賠償。雖然日本政府承認做錯事，但日本法院卻因"個人不能告政府"、"追訴時效已過"拒審。直到今天，大多數日本小孩及成年人都不知道這個悲劇。

　　2007 年，美國眾議院通過第 121 號決議，要求日本政府把慰安婦的真實史實加入教科書，但日本政府沒有這麼做。前國務卿希拉蕊柯林頓是慰安婦最堅強的支持者，她說"慰安婦"這個用詞太過虛偽，事實上她們是被強迫的性奴。

　　2011 年起，慰安婦的雕像在全世界各地樹立，雕像中一位年輕的女性握緊拳頭，憤怒地瞪著日本政府，因為它漠視自己的戰爭罪行。

　　2013 年，加州 Glendale 市樹立了一個慰安婦雕像「Glendale 和平紀念碑」。一個日本政府支持的原告提起訴訟，要求市政府把雕像移走，原告說，樹立這個雕像超越了市政府的權限，並干涉美國政府處理外交事務的權利。聯邦地方法院拒絕審理這個案子，原告上訴至第九巡迴法院，法官 Kim McLane Wardlaw 在判決中說，「建立這個雕像，是 Glendale 市在違反人權事件上表態，這是州政府和地方政府被賦予的基本權利。」Gingery v. City of Glendale, No.14-56440 (9th Cir. 2016).

1937

A Paper Daughter with Six Names

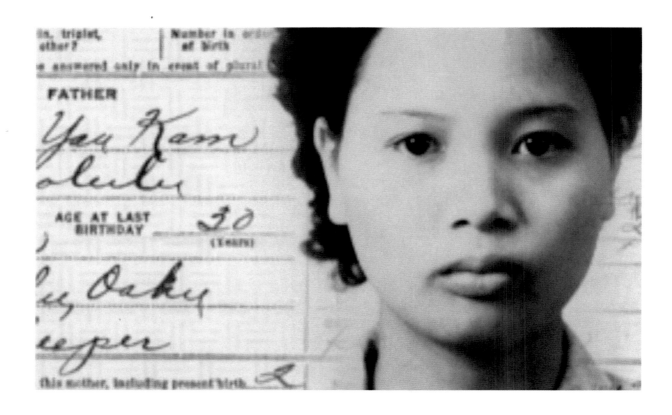

Louie Gum To was born in Zhongshan, China in 1920. During her life time, her name changed six times.

Her first name change happened in 1937 when she came to the U.S. during the Chinese Exclusion Era (1882-1943) when America banned Chinese from entering the country. One way to circumvent the discriminatory laws was to assume the identity of a deceased U.S. citizen.

Gum To's mother persuaded a family to let Gum To take their dead daughter's place. She then became Kam Sau Quon, a "paper daughter".

An America teacher gave her a new name, Lettie. When she married Thomas Wing Jue in 1945, her name became Lettie Jue. But Jue was Thomas' paper name as well. In 1952, he legally changed back to his real family surname, Lowe. Lettie was now Lettie Kam Lowe.

After Thomas passed away, Lettie married Abelardo Cooper and her name changed for the sixth time to Lettie Lowe Cooper. By this time, Lettie had become a successful business woman.

In 2015, her daughter Felicia Lowe produced Chinese Couplets, an acclaimed documentary about her mother's life. From paper daughter to successful entrepreneur, Lettie personified the American Dream.

對聯 Chinese Couplets
A film by Felicia Lowe

HOME   SCREENINGS   MEDIA   BUY DVDS   ABOUT   CONTACT

與君生別離   行行重行行

On and on, traveling on and on,
Far from you to live apart.
—Nineteen Old Poems

1937

「紙上女兒」雷金桃一生共有六個名字

雷金桃於 1920 年出生於廣東中山，她第一次改名是在 1937 年。當年因為排華法案，中國人來美的變通之道就是頂用死去的美國公民的身分，成千上萬的「紙上兒子」及「紙上女兒」就這樣誕生了。

雷金桃的母親找到了有年齡相近的女兒過世的家庭，同意她以女兒「甘秀群」的名義來美。入境不久，她的老師又給她取了英文名字 Lettie。

Lettie 後來冠夫姓 - 趙，成為 Lettie Jue「趙永信」。1952 年，她丈夫（也是紙上兒子）向法院申請改回他真正的姓氏 - 劉，她就成了「劉永信」。先生去世後她改嫁了，丈夫的姓是 Cooper，Lettie Cooper 後來成為一個很成功的商人。她於 2001 年過世。

2015 年她的女兒劉詠嫦以記錄片「中國對聯」來紀念她。紙上女兒 Lettie 一生艱苦奮鬥，總算實現了她的美國夢。

1968

The year the term "Chinese American" was born

Dr. Chang C. Chen in 50 years anniversary held for San Francisco State University Ethnic Studies program

If you have experienced the questions and answers below, you are Chinese American.

What are you? *American.*

I mean, where are you from? *Brooklyn.*

No, where are you really from? *Brooklyn.*

Well then, what country are your people from? *My people are from China, now what country are your people from?*

I am from America, of course.

1968 is considered the most turbulent year in American politics. With the Vietnam War, the assassinations of Martin Luther King, Jr. and Robert F. Kennedy, modern American liberalism became mainstream.

At the time, 17 years old Vicci Wong was a student at U.C. Berkeley. She and five other Asian Ph.D. candidates: Emma Gee, Yuji Ichioka, Victor Ichioka, Floyd Huen and Richard Aoki, tried to get involved in the civil rights movement, but found themselves caught between black and white. Not belonging to either, they met to discuss the problems they were facing. Previously, they were Oriental, but after that defining meeting, they identified themselves as Asian American.

They brought to light the welfare of Asian minorities by organizing the longest sit-in protest at U.C. Berkeley and San Francisco State University. They encouraged universities to set up Ethnic Studies departments.

The term Asian American grew to include Chinese, Japanese, Korean, Filipino, Thailand, Vietnamese, Indians, and other Asians. Life had never been easy for Chinese Americans. They suffered discrimination from the Chinese Exclusion Act since 1882, and the internment of 120,000 Japanese Americans during World War II, among many other obstacles.

By 2019, there were 5 million Chinese Americans, consisting of 1.3% of the total American population. Because of historical employment discrimination, the U.S. is currently home to more than 40,000 Chinese restaurants. This number is greater than all the MacDonald's, KFC, Pizza Hut, Taco Bell and Wendy's combined!

In a pair of cases, Ozawa v. United States (1922) and United States v. Bhagat Singh Thind (1923), the Supreme Court ruled that Asians were not "white persons". Second-generation Chinese Americans, however, could become U.S. citizens due to the birthright citizenship clause of the Fourteenth Amendment; this guarantee was confirmed by the Supreme Court in United States v. Wong Kim Ark (1898).

Even with citizenship, Chinese were not considered Americans.

The ongoing China-United States trade war since 2018 and the 2020 coronavirus pandemic worries many Chinese Americans. As China is seen as a threat, Chinese Americans fear they are targeted and hate crimes against them are on the rise. While the term Chinese American celebrates its 52nd birthday, many of them still wonder, "What does it take to become American? "

YOUR ASIAN WASN'T QUIET

She wasn't a model minority. Wasn't your Asian fantasy. Maybe chose a path other than motherhood. She speaks truth to power. This is what Asian America looks like. Get used to it. **NOT CREATED IN YOUR IMAGE**

AAPA cofounder Vicci Wong (right) with an unidentified mother and children at a Black Panther Party Free Huey rally on the steps of the Alameda Country Courthourse in Oakland, CA.

Student activist Vicci Wong in 2018

1968

「華裔美國人」今年五十二歲了！

如果你也經歷過以下的對話，那你應該是華裔美國人。

What are you? American
你是哪種人？ 我是美國人

I mean, where are you from? Brooklyn
我的意思是，你從哪來？ 布魯克林

No, where are you really from? Brooklyn
不，我的意思是你真的從哪來？ 布魯克林

Well then, what country are you from?
那你的族群是從哪個國家來？

My people are from China, now what country are your people from?
我的族群是從中國來。那你從哪來？

I am from America, of course.'
我當然來自美國！

1968 年是美國政壇起伏最大的一年，當時因為參與越戰，及黑人民權領袖金恩、羅伯甘迺迪被殺，群情激憤，民權主義從此成為美國社會的主流價值觀。

但是身處黑白兩界的華裔及亞裔卻很尷尬，不知道自己應該加入那個陣營。當年 17 歲的 Vicci Wong 正在柏克萊大學唸書，她找到了其他亞裔博士生 Emma

Gee, Yuji Ichioka, Floyd Huen, Richard Aoki, and Victor Ichioka，他們都想為民權運動提供亞裔的貢獻。他們在開會之前被稱為「東方人」，開會後他們決定從此就是「亞裔美國人」了。亞裔美國人包括從中國來的華裔、日裔、韓裔、菲裔、泰裔、越裔、印裔及其他從亞洲國家來的人，以來自中國的移民及其後代人數最多。

他們後來在柏克萊大學及舊金山州立大學展開了史上最長的靜坐抗議，成功的爭取到幾所大學成立「種族研究科系」，讓社會重視少數族裔的福祉。

在 Ozawa v. United States (1922) 及 United States v. Bhagat Singh Thind (1923) 兩案中，最高法院認定亞裔不是白人，但因為憲法第十四條修正案的「出生公民權」，第二代的華裔美國人可以成為公民，這個判決在 United States v. Wong Kim Ark (1898) 中被確認。

至 2019 年，華裔美國人人數為五百萬，組成美國 1.3% 的人口。華裔美國人的日子一向不好過，有 1882 年 1943 年長達六十年的排華法案、2018 年開始的中美貿易戰及 2020 年的新冠病毒大流行（川普總統竟稱之為" 中國病毒"）。川普一再宣稱中國是美國最大的敵人，讓華人處境危機四伏。

面對仇恨犯罪的日益增加，華裔美國人不盡感嘆，" 我們要怎樣才會被認為是美國人？"

1972

Cecilia Chiang sued San Francisco Culinary Workers' Union

On June 23, 1968, Cecilia Chiang opened the *Mandarin* in Ghirardelli Square in San Francisco. For the next 23 years, the *Mandarin* defined upscale Chinese dining.

George Chen was a waiter at the *Mandarin* in the late 1970s and he recalled, "Cecilia knew every customer by name. She would make the rounds of the dining room in her beautiful gowns and jewelry and would flash her big diamonds. You always wanted her to visit your tables, even you knew the check average was going up."

http://www.local2benefits.org/toc/ dex.html

In 1972, the San Francisco Culinary Workers' Union began targeting the *Mandarin* to force the restaurant to join the Union. They told Chiang that even the most famous Hollywood movie stars had to join and paid the Union dues.

To harass her, the Union gathered more than 300 demonstrators. They carried placards and distributed leaflets in front of the *Mandarin* during business hours, stopping restaurant food trucks from delivering and harassing patrons from entering the restaurant. The *Mandarin* was able to remain open during this turbulent period, because Chiang had all the deliveries made after midnight when the demonstrators retired for the day.

Chiang brought a libel suit against the Union in 1972 and won after seven years. However, both parties agreed to seal all the court records making them inaccessible to the public.

1972

江孫芸 訴 舊金山餐飲工會

1968 年 6 月 23 日，江孫芸的福祿壽餐廳在舊金山吉拉德里廣場開幕，在隨後的 23 年裡，福祿壽成了最高端中國餐飲的代表。

一位 1970 年代末在福祿壽餐廳工作的侍應生回憶，「江孫芸能記住所有客人的名字，她在餐桌之間穿梭自如，穿著華麗的禮服、帶著名貴珠寶，四處展示她的大鑽石，而每個客人都希望她能來自己這桌，他們也知道這意味著更多的消費。」

1972 年舊金山餐飲從業人員工會注意到了福祿壽餐廳，強烈要求他們參加工會。工會代表告訴江孫芸，連最有名的好萊塢明星都得參加工會、繳會費，福祿壽也不能例外。

江孫芸一再婉拒，於是工會找了 300 多人在福祿壽餐廳前舉牌抗議，說福祿壽是血汗餐館，抗議者在餐廳開業時阻擋送貨車進入，騷擾來用餐的客人，甚至還對江孫芸使用暴力，把她壓在地上暴打，對當時在現場目睹的兒子，產生了不可磨滅的痛苦影響。但福祿壽卻能在這段艱困的日子裡繼續開業，因為江孫芸請所有的送貨公司都在夜裡 12 點之後再送貨，那時工會的人下班了。

1972 年，江孫芸對工會提起了毀謗之訴，七年後她贏得了這場官司。工會覺得很丟臉，最後雙方達成協議，密封所有關於本案的法院文件，所以現在在法院資料庫查不到本案的資料。

1974

Dr. March Fong Eu was a toilette-smashing trailblazer

In 1969, Oakland Assemblywoman March Fong Eu took a sledgehammer to a porcelain toilet on the steps of the State Capitol Building in Sacramento, California. Symbolically smashing chains, Dr. Eu's career spanned decades in which she shattered barriers for women, and particularly for Chinese American women.

Dr. Eu was raised in the back of a Chinese laundromat in San Francisco. When she went to high school, a guidance counselor told her that no school would hire a Chinese woman. Her parents had no perception of her possibilities either, but Dr. Eu was not deterred by what other people thought.

Dr. Eu earned a doctorate in education from Stanford University. She worked as a dental hygienist and spent three terms on the Alameda County Board of Education. In 1966, she won an Assembly seat from a district that included Oakland and Castro Valley.

Dr. Eu's signature issue, a statewide ban on pay toilets in public buildings, was also a matter of gender fairness. She argued that pay toilets symbolized secondhand status for women since there was no charge for public urinals. Her sledgehammer assault on the toilet attracted attention across the nation.

In 1974, Governor Ronald Reagan signed the bill that banned pay public toilets, just six weeks before voters elected her with a record of 3.4 million votes to become Secretary of State. She was unbeatable in the next four re-elections.

In 1976, she became the first woman to serve as Acting Governor of California while Governor Jerry Brown was out of the state.

In 1994, she was nominated as ambassador to Micronesia by President Clinton, a post she held for two years until 1996.

In 2019, she was the first woman to have a State Building named after her: March Fong Eu Secretary of State building in Sacramento.

Dr. Eu introduced many voter innovations during her twenty years as Secretary of State. These include voter registration by mail, absentee ballots, posting results on the internet and candidate statements in ballot pamphlets.

She was a true trailblazer, from being the first Chinese American woman elected to the state legislature, to serving nearly 20 years as California's first female Secretary of State. Dr. Eu did not call herself a feminist, but she bristled at restrictions on women and those who aimed at breaking the glass ceiling.

1974

先驅者 -- 加州首位華裔女州務卿余江月桂

余江月桂在第一代移民的父母洗衣店裡長大，出身寒微的她，面對當時社會嚴重的性別和種族歧視，力爭上游，打破多個玻璃天花板，成為華裔女性從政的先驅。

她在唸中學時，老師跟她說，沒有學校會聘請中國女性，余江月桂的父母對她也沒抱任何期望，但這些都沒有阻止她考上加州大學柏克萊分校，並在斯坦福大學獲得博士學位。

余江月桂曾擔任牙醫助理三年，之後她在加州阿拉米達教育局任職，1966年，她當選州議員。她任內主張男女平權，最為人稱道的是禁止加州公共建築物裡的女廁收費，因為使用男廁免費，使用女廁則要付費，是明顯的性別歧視。

1969 年 4 月，身為州議員的她在州政府的台階上，拿著一把大錘，公然把馬桶擊碎，她這麼一錘，不但吸引了全美媒體的瘋狂報導，也在讓她在六個禮拜之後，以破紀錄的 3.4 百萬票登上了州務卿的寶座。1974 年，加州州長雷根簽署禁止公廁收費的法律。

余江月桂成為加州首位華裔和首位女性州務卿，也是當時職位最高的華裔民選官員。她隨後連任 4 次，任期長達 19 年。1994 年，克林頓總統委任她為密克羅尼西亞大使，1996 年任滿回美。

余江月桂一生充滿傳奇，締造了很多第一，她是：
• 第一位獲任阿拉米達學區委員會主席的華裔女性、
• 第一位擔任加州議員的華裔女性、
• 第一位當選為加州州務卿的華裔女性、

• 第一位當選為加州世界貿易委員會主席的華裔女性、

• 第一位代理加州州長的華裔女性。

她在 19 年州務卿任內的創新，包括：

• 選民可以通訊登記、

• 提供缺席選票、

• 在網路上公佈選舉結果、

• 在選票上列入候選人政見。

2019 年，加州州務大樓正式命名為 **March Fong Eu 州務卿大樓**，這是首次加州政府大樓以女性名字命名。

余江月桂從未自稱女權運動者，但她絕不放過任何對女性的性別限制，成為女性打破玻璃天花板最重要的角色典範。

1981

Lilian Sing is the first Chinese-American female judge in Northern California

Judge Sing was born in Shanghai and came to United States at age fifteen. She was appointed to the San Francisco Municipal Court in 1981 by Governor Jerry Brown and in 1996, she was elected to the San Francisco Superior Court. She achieved the distinction of being the only sitting judge who had presided in every court division of the San Francisco trial court system. Presiding Judge Teri L. Jackson said, "Judge Sing has worked tirelessly for fairness and justice, and for those who did not have a voice. She is the ultimate role model."

When Judge Sing retired in 2015, she and Judge Julie Tang co-founded the *Comfort Women Justice Coalition* and successfully installed the first *Comfort Women Memorial* in a major city, San Francisco, in the United States.

In 2018 and 2019, Lillian and Julie traveled to Seoul, South Korea to attend a conference hosted by the ICJN *(International Committee of Joint Nominators)* to urge *UNESCO (United Nations Educational, Scientific and Cultural Organization)* to register *The 1,149 Voices of the Comfort Women* documents into its *Memory of World Registry (MoW)*. Unfortunately, UNESCO has buckled under Japan's pressure and has postponed its decision twice.

Sing said it is crucial that UNESCO is not bullied by Japan. The Comfort Women history cannot be white-washed and erased. It must be told truthfully.

Lillian Sing was sworn in by the first female California Supreme Court Justice, Rose Elizabeth Bird (1981)

San Francisco's Comfort Women Memorial

1981

郭麗蓮是北加州第一位華人女法官

郭麗蓮出生於上海，15 歲赴美留學，後來成為美國執業律師。

1981 年她獲得加州州長布朗提名，成為舊金山市立法院女法官，也是北加州第一位華裔高等法院女法官。1996 年，她經競選，成為民選的舊金山高等法院法官。她回憶，「我當時心裡很害怕，如果我做不好，不單只是影響個人，還會影響到未來華裔女法官的發展。」舊金山審判庭法官 Teri L. Jackson 後來說，「在郭麗蓮 34 年的法官生涯裡，她從不倦怠的為公平和正義奮鬥，為沒有聲音的人發音，她是最佳的人格典範。」

她於 2015 年退休，全心投入為華人服務，同時致力為二戰遭日軍凌虐的慰安婦請命。當時第二次世界大戰已結束 70 年，郭麗蓮說她難以相信日本至今仍拒絕承認日軍在二戰期間的殘酷行為，也否認曾逼迫無數年輕女性淪為慰安婦。於是她與另一位退休女法官鄧孟詩成立「*慰安婦正義聯盟*」，經過千辛萬苦，總算在舊金山豎立了「*慰安婦紀念碑*」。

2018 年及 2019 年，郭麗蓮及鄧孟詩兩位女法官到漢城參加「*國際聯合提名人委員會*」（ICJN）的會議，敦促聯合國教科文組織在它的「*世界記憶計劃*」中註冊「*1149 個慰安婦的聲音*」，但因日本強烈反對，教科文組織在壓力下兩次推延做出決定。

郭麗蓮法官再三強調，慰安婦的歷史不能被抹去，它必須被真實的陳述，才能防止悲劇再次發生。

1989

Helen Liu v. Republic of China, *892 F.2d 1419 (1989)*

Helen Liu lived with her husband, Henry Liu, and their son in Daly City, California. Henry was the U.S. correspondent of the Taiwan Daily and his articles were fiercely critical of Chiang Ching-kuo's regime in Taiwan.

On October 15, 1984, Henry was murdered in his garage, shot three times at close range, and his assailants fled the scene.

The assassination was planned by Chen Chi-li, leader of the Bamboo Union Triad in Taiwan, and carried out by two Union members, Wu Tun and Tung Kuei-sen. Chen was acting on the request of the head of Taiwan's Military Intelligence Bureau, Vice Admiral Wang Hsi-ling, who wanted to teach Liu a lesson. Since the killers had no formal training, they left fingerprints everywhere and soon afterwards, the U.S. Federal Bureau of Investigation (FBI) asked Taiwan to provide information of the killers.

This case sent shockwaves around the world, because a foreign government dared to send killers to murder an American citizen on American soil. In 1985, the House of Representatives passed a non-binding resolution urging Taiwan to remand custody of the murder suspects to the United States for trial.

Bowing to pressure from the U.S., Taiwan authorities arrested Chen and Wu, along with 300 other members of the Bamboo Union during a government crackdown on organized crime. Chen and Wu served six years. Wang, who faced a military tribunal, also served six years.

Helen Liu filed a wrongful death lawsuit in the United States District Court, Northern District of California against Taiwan and the six named conspirators, alleging that her husband's murder had been arranged by Taiwanese officials acting in an official capacity.

Although the suit survived an early motion to dismiss on the *act of state* grounds, Judge Eugene F. Lynch dropped Taiwan from the suit in 1987 based on a Taiwan military tribunal's conclusion that Wang did not act on behalf of the Taiwan government.

The Ninth Circuit Court of Appeals reversed Lynch's decision, ruling in Liu v Republic of China (Taiwan) that Taiwan government was liable under *the doctrine of respondeat superior*, a petition for certiorari from the Taiwan government to the U.S.

Supreme Court was subsequently rejected. The suit was finally settled out of court and Helen received $1.45 million settlement.

Helen Liu eulogized her husband and said that he gave his life in exchange for the democratization of Taiwan. His death was honorable and dignified.

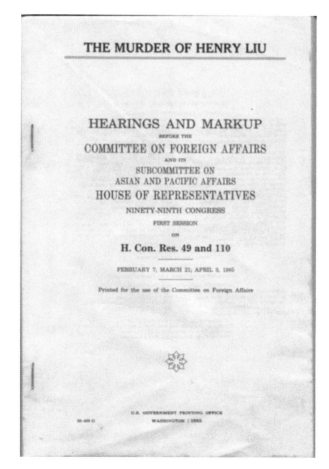

THE MURDER OF HENRY LIU

HEARINGS AND MARKUP
BEFORE THE
COMMITTEE ON FOREIGN AFFAIRS
AND ITS
SUBCOMMITTEE ON
ASIAN AND PACIFIC AFFAIRS
HOUSE OF REPRESENTATIVES

NINETY-NINTH CONGRESS

FIRST SESSION

ON

H. Con. Res. 49 and 110

FEBRUARY 7; MARCH 21; APRIL 3, 1985

Printed for the use of the Committee on Foreign Affairs

U.S. GOVERNMENT PRINTING OFFICE
WASHINGTON : 1985

1989

崔蓉芝 訴 中華民國 *892 F.2d 1419*

1963 年，崔蓉芝在台北嫁給劉宜良，劉宜良的筆名是江南，他那時在很多雜誌上寫文章，文章包括了他博士論文的題材 -- 蔣經國傳。

當時台灣在戒嚴狀態下，劉宜良的文章卻對國民黨政權諸多批評，劉的長官常被警備總部叫去談話，劉宜良則是經常覺得有人跟蹤他。因為擔心會被限制出境，所以在 1967 年，劉宜良以台灣日報駐美特派員身份，與崔蓉芝及幼兒移居美國。

他們在美國舊金山開禮品店，1984 年 10 月 15 日上午，江南在 Daly City 的住所被台灣國防部情報局派來的兩位殺手槍殺。因為殺手沒經過訓練，四處留下線索，美國 FBI 很快的就循線跟台灣要人了。

這個案子在美國被廣泛的報導，因為外國政府竟然敢派殺手來美國境內謀殺美國公民，是可忍，孰不可忍？美國眾議院還為此舉辦了一次公聽會，主題是 The Murder of Henry Liu， 要求台灣政府把謀殺犯交還美國審判。

台灣政府迫不得已，只好以「一清專案」的名義，把兩個竹聯幫殺手逮捕並判處無期徒刑，但他們六年後就被假釋，出獄後還自誇在獄中因為「愛國」行為享受貴賓待遇，可以抽菸、吃龍蝦。情報局局長汪希苓也被判無期徒刑，坐牢六年之後出獄。

江南被殺後，他的朋友們組了「江南事件委員會」，協助崔蓉芝於 1988 年在舊金山高等法院向台灣政府提告，要台灣為劉宜良的不當致死負責。台灣政府辯稱，台灣法院已對江南謀殺案做出了刑事判決，根據「國家行為原則」(The Act of State doctrine) 崔蓉芝無權揭發台灣法院判決的內幕，而且情報局長汪希苓的作為也不在他工作權限內，舊金山地方法院同意台灣的說法，崔蓉芝隨即上訴至加州第九巡迴上訴法院。

1989 年 12 月 29 日，第九巡迴法院推翻地方法院判決，宣示「國家行為原則」並不是自動就給一個外國國家免訴權，特別是當它命令殺手來美國境內謀殺美國公民時。本案的殺手都自認是在為國家效力，懲罰對蔣經國總統不敬的叛徒，所以汪希苓的作為也在他的職權之內，因此台灣政府必須依照加州的「雇主責任」法理，為劉宜良之死負責。

崔蓉芝後來收到台灣政府賠償她的 1 百 45 萬美元。

名作家及歷史學家柏楊評論，江南奉獻生命和鮮血，化做壓死蔣家政權的最後一根稻草，蔣家政權從此一蹶不振，蔣經國於 1985 年透過美國時代週刊表示，蔣家人今後不能也不會參選總統。

崔蓉芝感嘆，江南是用生命換來台灣的民主化，雖逝猶榮。

1991

Dr. Shuping Wang was a public health histleblower

Dr. Shuping Wang was a well-known public health whistleblower in China. She exposed the poor practices that led to the spread of hepatitis C and HIV in the 1990s, saving tens of thousands of lives.

A specialist in hepatitis, Dr. Wang was assigned to a plasma collection station in Zhoukou City, Henan Province in 1991. She discovered many unsafe practices, such as accepting blood plasma donors who were already infected with hepatitis C. She implored officials at the site to change the collection practices, but was turned down because of cost.

Undeterred, Dr. Wang took her concerns to the Ministry of Health in Beijing, which began to require hepatitis C screening for blood plasma donors in 1993. She continued to inspect facilities elsewhere in the region and found similar cross-contamination.

Using her own resources, her investigation found that the hepatitis C antibody positive rate to be as high as 84.3% and HIV infection rate, 13%. She wrote, "I know that hepatitis C and HIV had the same routes of infection, I wanted to directly monitor it and prevent it." She again took the samples to Beijing, trying to convince them to let her monitor and prevent HIV-AIDS from spreading. She was dismissed by local and provincial health leaders who were embarrassed by her revelations.

A retired leader of the Health Bureau smashed the sign of her testing site with a baton, destroyed her equipment--and when she tried to stop him, he struck her.

In 1996, Dr. Wang's wish was granted and collection sites begin administering HIV testing for donors. But her clinical testing center was ultimately closed. In 2001, with the help of an American reporter, she moved to the U.S.

By 2001, a senior Chinese government official conceded for the first time that China had a very serious epidemic of HIV-AIDS, and affirmed that more than half a million citizens in central China may have been infected by HIV due to poor collection practices which Wang had exposed.

On September 5, 2019, a play entitled *The King of Hell's Palace* was shown in London's Hampstead Theater. The play was based on the story of the HIV epidemic in the Zhoukou region and Dr. Wang's whistleblowing.

Dr. Wang said Chinese police intimidated her family and friends, hoping to stop the play from showing. But she said, even after all this time, she will still not be silenced.

Dr. Wang passed away suddenly in Salt Lake City on September 21, 2019. After Dr. Wang's death, David Cowhig, a former U.S. Foreign Service officer in Beijing wrote, "Now it can be told: Shuping Wang…was the single most important source for U.S. officials seeking to understand and curb the HIV epidemic in China."

1991

王淑平醫生揭發了中國愛滋傳染的真相

王淑平醫生是一位著名的吹哨人,她揭露了華中地區因為獻血者篩選過程的缺失,導致 1990 年間丙型肝炎及愛滋病疫情的快速傳染。因為王醫生的勇氣及自我犧牲的精神,成千上萬的人免於受到愛滋病的感染。

王醫生是肝病治療的專家。1991 年,她被分配到河南省周口市的一個獻血站工作,她發現在當地的獻血過程中存在許多問題,例如丙型肝炎患者仍然可以獻血等等,她向獻血站的領導懇求,希望他們能改進獻血者的篩選,但被拒絕了,他們的理由是這樣做會增加成本。但王醫生並未退縮,她把她的顧慮直接告訴了北京的衛生部,1993 年衛生部規定,所有獻血者都要接受丙型肝炎檢測。

王醫生繼續檢查附近地區的獻血站,發現仍有同樣的交叉感染問題。她乾脆自己出資幫助檢測,結果發現 84.3% 的血液標本中含有丙型肝炎的抗體,其中 13% 的標本可能來自愛滋病感染者。王醫生知道丙型肝炎和愛滋病是經過同樣的途徑感染,她希望能夠說服北京政府相關部門,讓自己追蹤和防止這兩種疾病的傳播。

在此同時,她卻受到了地區及省級衛生部門領導的冷言冷語,他們認為她的調查結果否定了他們的工作,甚至有個退休的衛生局領導,用棍子把她檢驗站的標誌打爛,毀損她的儀器,當她試圖阻止時,還用棍子打她。

在王醫生的努力下,1996 年,獻血站終於被迫關門了。當它重新開門時,新的規定是獻血者必須接受愛滋病的檢測,王醫生成功了,但她的檢驗中心也被關閉了,她丟掉了工作、丈夫與她離了婚,2001 年,她終於在一位美國記者協助下移民到美國。

2001 年，中國政府總算承認了愛滋病疫情在境內快速增長的事實，有超過五十萬華中地區的人民，因為捐血者篩選過程的缺失，感染了愛滋病，可悲的是這是發生在王醫生提出這個問題十年以後。

2019 年 9 月 5 日，倫敦 Hampstead 戲院演出「地獄王的皇宮」。劇情描述河南周口市的愛滋疫情和王醫生作為吹哨人的故事。王醫生說，中國員警又找上她的家人和朋友了，要求這齣戲不要演出，但王醫生說，雖然經歷了這麼長的時間，但她是不可能被噤聲的。

2019 年 9 月 21 日，王淑平醫生於美國猶他州鹽湖城驟逝。

王醫生去逝後，一位 1990 年代在北京美國大使館工作的外交官在他的博客上寫道，「現在我終於能說了，王淑平醫生是當時美國官員想瞭解及阻止中國愛滋疫情爆發唯一的、最重要的消息來源。」

1991

Julie Tang is the first Chinese-American female elected judge of the San Francisco Municipal Court

Born in Hong Kong, Judge Tang came to the United States as a teenager. She was

a deputy District Attorney for eight years before being elected to the municipal court in 1991. Tang later took on two difficult areas of domestic violence and controlled substance cases, and has shown tremendous compassion dealing with those who have come before her. "If you like people, it's the kind of court you want to work in." Tang said, "You're not just the woman in the black robe on the bench."

Judge Tang retired in 2014. She and Judge Lillian Sing co-founded the *Comfort*

Women Justice Coalition and successfully installed the first *Comfort Women Memorial* in a major city, San Francisco in United States in 2017. It was a hard-fought battle.

The Mayor of Osaka, Japan had threatened to end its sister-city relationship with San Francisco if Mayor Ed Lee designated the new monument as city property. Lee did just that on November 22, 2017.

Judge Tang continues to promote the history and education of the Comfort Women and other atrocities committed by the Japanese Armed Forces during WWII. She wants to make sure these crimes will not be repeated. Tang said, "History repeats itself when it isn't remembered."

Judges Lillian Sing and Julie Tang with a Chinese
Comfort Woman from Hainan in 2015

1991

鄧孟詩成為舊金山第一位民選法官

鄧孟詩出生於香港，十餘歲時移民美國，柏克萊大學法學院畢業，獲得律師資格。1983年起，鄧孟詩擔任代理檢察官，於1991年被選為舊金山市立法院法官。

鄧法官主持過兩類挑戰很大的案件：家暴案和管制藥物案，她對受審者展現極大的同情心，她說，「如果你喜歡跟人相處，法院就是你的地方。我不只是一個穿著黑袍、坐在法官席上的女性。」

舊金山市的「*慰安婦紀念雕像*」來之不易。大阪市長吉村洋文曾威脅舊金山市長，如果該市豎立慰安婦紀念碑，就要取消大阪和舊金山的姊妹市關係。舊金山市長李孟賢回答，「慰安婦雕像一事無交涉餘地。」郭麗蓮法官說，放置慰安婦紀念碑的目的是要提醒犯罪者認錯。

2018年和2019年，她和郭麗蓮法官到了漢城，要求聯合國教科文組織註冊「*1149個慰安婦的聲音*」於「*世界記憶註冊*」中，但因為日本的強烈反對，教科文組織延遲了兩次還不肯決定。

鄧法官繼續推廣及教育年輕人關於慰安婦及其他日本軍隊在第二次世界大戰的罪行，她說，「人類若要確定不再重複這種罪行，就要記住這段歷史。」

2004

Heather Fong: First Chinese American Woman Chief of Police in San Francisco

Heather Fong grew up in San Francisco. Her father owned a Chinese grocery store in Oakland, and her mother was a legal secretary. In high school, Fong met a visiting police officer and was inspired to become a police officer herself. She graduated from the Police Academy in 1977 and was still in probationary training when she received orders to help with a major Chinatown shooting.

Fong's Chinese language skills were desperately needed in the investigation of *the Golden Dragon Restaurant Massacre* on September 4, 1977. As the result of the violent encounter of two Chinatown gangs, five people were dead and eleven wounded--all innocent bystanders. Police later called it the worst massacre in San Francisco history. The public outrage led to the formation of *San Francisco Police Gang Task Force*. The city started to pay greater attention to the problems of Chinatown.

To solve the case, Fong painstakingly translated hundreds of hours of taped conversations from Cantonese into English and was a major force that led to several convictions and lengthy prison sentences.

Fong was the first Chinese American woman police officer in San Francisco. In the 1970s, she struggled in a field that was notorious for racial and sexual discrimination. She won successive promotions through her determination to work harder than anyone else at the job.

On April 14, 2004, Fong was appointed Chief of Police of San Francisco by Mayor Gavin Newsom, becoming the first Chinese American woman to head a major metropolitan city police force. She retired from the force in 2009.

In 2014, Heather Fong became the Assistant Secretary of the Department of Homeland Security (DHS) for State and Local Law Enforcement. She retired from DHS in 2018.

2004

方宇文是第一位華人女性警察局長

方宇文在舊金山長大，父親曾在奧克蘭經營中國雜貨店，母親從事法務助理。沈默寡言的方宇文說自己一向很少出門或去逛街，難以想像她這樣的個性後來會成為執法的警察。方宇文在高中時，碰到一位來校訪問的警察，受到激勵，決定自己將來也要做警察。

1977 年 9 月 4 日，她從警察學校畢業，正在受訓，突然收到電話，舊金山中國城的金龍大酒家發生了慘絕人寰的屠殺案，華人幫派在餐廳內持槍屠殺，導致 5 位無辜的食客死亡，11 人受傷，急需懂得中文的警察來辦案。

這樁血腥暴力的幫派仇殺事件，引起眾怒，市政府不得不成立*舊金山警察幫派工作小組*，並開始重視中國城內的諸多問題。為了解決這個案子，方宇文努力不懈的把幾百個小時的訪問錄音從廣東話翻譯成英文，她是本案最後能破案及定罪的最大功臣。

方宇文是第一位華人女性警察，在 1970 年代，她身處這個種族及性別歧視最嚴重的行業裡，努力工作、力爭上游。

2004 年，舊金山市長紐森任命她為該市有史以來第一位女性警察局長，她是第一位在美國大都會城市中擔任警察局長的華人女性。

她最為中國城居民津津樂道的，是她每年都會參加中國城安老自助處舉辦的感恩節敬老活動，為華裔老人送感恩火雞餐到家，至今數十餘年。方宇文於 2009 年從舊金山警察局退休。

2014 年，方宇文成為美國國土安全部助理部長，負責與各州各市的警察局聯絡及溝通，她於 2018 年從國土安全部退休。

2012

Ellen Pao exposing a culture of prevalent workplace discrimination

In 2007, Ellen Pao became a junior partner at Kleiner Perkins, a major venture capital firm headquartered in Silicon Valley. Pao led the firm's expansion into China. After several years, she was passed over for a senior partner position.

In 2012, Ellen Pao filed a gender discrimination suit against Kleiner Perkins. The case went to trial in 2015 and garnered national attention regarding the issue of gender discrimination in the workplace. The Silicon Valley culture is that of widespread gender discrimination and an under-representation of women in venture capital.

Pao alleged that promotions were unfairly given to men ahead of women, whose input were easily dismissed. Women who reported cases of sexual harassment did not receive adequate support. However, the jury decided the case in favor of Kleiner Perkins on all counts.

Still, in 2019, only 15% of funding for U.S. tech start-ups go to teams with one or more female founders. Fewer than 10% of venture capitalists are women. The numbers have plateaued in the past four years since Ellen Pao's landmark case.

Discrimination cases in the U.S. are rare. In 2017's *"Rights on Trial: How Workplace Discrimination Law Perpetuates Inequality"*, author Ellen Berrey found that in nearly 2000 employment discrimination cases, most were thrown out or settled. The cost of litigation and adversarial process proves too big a barrier for the employees, only 6% of the cases went to trial and two-thirds plaintiffs failed.

Ellen Pao was far from a perfect plaintiff, but more power to her for putting herself painfully on the line to expose so much that is wrong with U.S. corporate culture. Although Pao lost the case, she gave many women the strength to speak out against the same mistreatment.

2012

鮑康如揭發職場性別歧視

2007 年，鮑康如是矽谷凱鵬華盈創業投資公司的初級合夥人，她主導公司在中國開拓業務，成績可觀，但幾年後，她並沒有被晉升為高級合夥人。

2012 年，鮑康如對凱鵬華盈提起性別歧視之訴，2015 年全案進入審判，她說在矽谷的創業投資公司中，性別歧視相當普遍，高階女性主管也特別少，她的控訴引起了全國的注目。鮑康如說，在升遷時，男性都會排在女性的前面，而女性所提出的建議也會被主管漠視，女性在揭發性騷擾時，一般得不到應有的情緒支持。但最後陪審團在所有的爭議點上，都判決凱鵬華盈勝訴。

直到 2019 年，美國只有 15% 女性發起的科技初創公司獲得資金挹注，少於 10% 的創業投資人是女性，在鮑康如的案子曝光後，創業投資公司幾乎全面停止雇用女性。

在美國提告歧視的案子很少，真相正如 2017 年的一本書 ”*審判的權利 -- 職場性別歧視的法律助長不平等*” 作者所說，在近 2000 個職場歧視訴訟中，絕大部分的結局是和解或是被法官駁回，鉅額的訴訟費及冗長的程序，對一般拿薪水的員工來說實在是太昂貴了。只有 6% 的案子最後進入審判，但三分之二的原告都輸了。

鮑康如不是一位最理想的原告，但她願意把自己放在第一線上，痛苦的暴露了美國公司偏頗的性別文化，她輸了訴訟，卻帶給其他女性揭發不公不義的勇氣。

2014

Sherry Chen was wrongfully accused spying for China

Sherry Chen moved to the U.S. from China in 1992 and became a citizen in 1997. She worked as a hydrologist for the National Weather Service (NWS) at the Ohio River Forecast Center in Wilmington, Ohio. NWS' data and products form a national database and infrastructure used by the global community.

Chen was a stellar employee who received many accolades for her work forecasting flood models for the Ohio River and its tributaries.

In 2012, Debbie Lee, a Caucasian co-worker accused Chen of spying for China. On October 20, 2014, six FBI agents took Sherry Chen away in handcuffs in front of her colleagues. The charges included stealing data, intentionally exceeding authorized access to a database, and lying to investigators. The punishment carried twenty-five years in jail and $1M in fines.

Five weeks later, prosecutors dropped all the charges without explanation or apology.

Despite the dropping of charges, the NWS fired her in March 2015. The U.S. Merit Systems Protection Board Judge Michele Szary reviewed the firing and found that officials buried evidence that would have cleared Chen. She ordered the Commerce Department to reinstate Chen, and to pay her salary and legal fees. The Commerce Department appealed this ruling on June 18, 2018.

The appeal has not been heard yet, but in the meantime, she has not returned to work at the NWS. Without fresh arguments, the appeal is, in effect, a delaying tactic.

Justice delayed is justice denied.

On January 18, 2019, Sherry Chen filed a civil lawsuit against the U.S. government for malicious prosecution and false arrest in the District Court for the Southern District of Ohio.

Sherry Chen's informer, Debbie Lee, has since been promoted to the Department of Commerce in charge of National Weather Service and has not offered a word of apology.

2014

水文專家陳霞芬被誣告為中國間諜

1992 年陳霞芬從中國移民美國，1997 年成為美國公民。她在美國商業部下屬的國家海洋和大氣管理局 (NWS) 做水文專家。NWS 的資料是全國性的資料庫，全世界皆可下載使用。

陳霞芬是位優秀的公務員，她的預測水流模式曾多次被表揚。2012 年，她的同事 Debbie Lee 告密說她是間諜，2014 年 10 月 20 日，六個聯邦調查局探員在陳霞芬同事面前，用手銬把她帶走，罪名包括竊取政府機密數據、非法下載敏感資料、對調查人員說謊等八項罪名，如果證實，她可被判入獄 25 年及罰款 1 百萬美元。

2015 年 3 月，在開庭前夕，檢察官突然撤銷所有對她的指控，沒有解釋、也沒有道歉。儘管如此，她的雇主 NWS 卻仍將她解僱。

2017 年 3 月，陳霞芬提起民事訴訟，起訴美國商業部就業歧視。2018 年 4 月 24 日，美國績效系統保護委員會首席行政法官裁定，商業部沒有任何理由解僱她，認定她是嚴重不公行為的受害者，命令商業部即刻將她復職，並支付她原應得的薪水及律師費。

2018 年 6 月 18 日，商業部就法官的裁定提起上訴，雖然他們沒有新的事證，但全案因此被拖延至今，尚未開庭。

2019 年 1 月，陳霞芬在俄亥俄州南區聯邦法院控告美國政府惡意起訴及錯誤逮捕。當年誣告陳霞芬的 Debbie Lee 卻被升官，現在成了商業部國家氣象局的主管，她尚未向陳霞芬就她的誣告道歉。

對陳霞芬來說，遲來的正義就不是正義了。

2017

A Chinese American woman in the #MeToo movement

Rowena Chiu, Harvey Weinstein's former assistant   "He told me he liked Chinese girls"

On October 5, 2017, *New York Times* reporters *Jodi Kantor* and *Megan Twohey* broke the *Harvey Weinstein* story. They aired allegations against the powerful American film producer that had been piling up for thirty years. Their report, along with subsequent reports, were based on scores of interviews with actresses and current and former employees, and documented a tangled web of bullying tactics, confidential settlements, cover-ups across decades around the world.

Kantor and Twohey watched with astonishment as a dam wall broke. As a result of a tidal wave of response, not only did they receive the 2018 Pulitzer Prize for Public Service, but they also published a book, *"She Said"* which lifted the lid on many secret stories, encouraging women all over the world to speak up about similar experiences. Their work ignited the # *MeToo* movement.

Sexual harassment in the workplace was finally brought to public attention, and Harvey Weinsteinwas accused of rape, sexual abuse and sexual assault for over thirty years by more than 130 women. He was found guilty by a New York States Supreme and sentenced to twenty-three years in prison, he is now at the Wende Correctional Facility where he is known as inmate No. 20B0584. He is still awaiting a second trial in Los Angeles for further alleged sexual offences.

Chinese American women were not spared from Weinstein's evil deeds. In 1998, 24-year-old *Rowena Chiu* had just graduated from Oxford University. She was passionate about starting a career in the film industry and elated to be hired as Assistant to Harvey Weinstein at Miramax London. Yet, weeks later, she found herself pushed against a bed by her boss. Weinstein told her that he had never 'had a Chinese girl before'. She recalls him saying, "Chinese girls keep secrets".

Rowena came from a traditional Chinese Christian family. She told her colleague *Zelda Perkins* about these events. Zelda was outraged, and both young women made a pact to quit their jobs and expose Weinstein. Zelda confronted her boss and told him that such behavior had to stop. Weinstein's lawyer pressured the two young women to sign nondisclosure agreements. Rowena kept her silence for 21 years, until the *#MeToo* movement was ignited.

Originally started as a grassroots effort by activist *Tarana Burke* more than 10 years ago, and set ablaze after a tweet by actress *Alyssa Milano*, "If you have been sexually harassed or assaulted, write *"me too"* as a reply to this tweet." Those two simple words have become a viral rallying cry for millions of women, who are fed up with the blatant abuse of power.

Recent study found that the *#MeToo* hashtag was used more than 19 million times on Twitter since Milano's initial tweet. Women from all over the world shared their painful memories of being sexually assaulted and raped. This movement had resulted in many powerful men losing their jobs.

After waiting twenty-one years for justice, *Rowena Chiu* finally broke her silence. She said, "We have a responsibility to speak up, so that when our daughters enter the workplace and encounter similar challenges, they will have options – they will know what to do, what to say, and which resources are available to them. In short, they can draw upon the strength of women who have spoken up before them.

The following is a list of Weinstein's victims who said, "Me too!"

Victims of Weinstein's Sexual Harassment or Assault

1. Amber Anderson, actress
2. Lysette Anthony, actress
3. Asia Argento, actress and director
4. Rosanna Arquette, actress
5. Jessica Barth, actress
6. Kate Beckinsale, actress
7. Juls Bindi, massage therapist
8. Cate Blanchett, actress
9. Helena Bonham Carter, actress
10. Zoë Brock, model
11. Cynthia Burr, actress
12. Liza Campbell, writer and artist
13. Alexandra Canosa, producer
14. Rowena Chiu, Weinstein employee
15. Marisa Coughlan, actress and writer
16. Hope Exiner d'Amore, Weinstein employee
17. Florence Darel, actress
18. Wedil David, actress
19. Emma de Caunes, actress
20. Paz de la Huerta, actress
21. Juliana De Paula, model
22. Cara Delevingne, actress and model
23. Sophie Dix, actress
24. Jane Doe, model and aspiring actress
25. Lacey Dorn, actress and filmmaker
26. Kaitlin Doubleday, actress
27. Caitlin Dulaney, actress
28. Dawn Dunning, actress
29. Lina Esco, actress and director
30. Alice Evans, actress
31. Lucia Evans, formerly Lucia Stoller, actress
32. Angie Everhart, model and actress
33. Claire Forlani, actress
34. Romola Garai, actress
35. Louisette Geiss, screenwriter and actress
36. Louise Godbold, nonprofit organization director
37. Judith Godrèche, actress
38. Trish Goff, former model, actress, and real estate broker

39. Larissa Gomes, actress

40. Heather Graham, actress

41. Eva Green, actress

42. Ambra Gutierrez, formerly Ambra Battilana, model

43. Mimi Haleyi, former production assistant

44. Daryl Hannah, actress

45. Salma Hayek, actress and producer

46. Lena Headey, actress

47. Anne Heche, actress

48. Lauren Holly, actress

49. Dominique Huett, actress

50. Amy Israel, Miramax executive

51. Angelina Jolie, actress and director

52. Ashley Judd, actress and political activist

53. Minka Kelly, actress

54. Katherine Kendall, actress

55. Heather Kerr, actress

56. Mia Kirshner, actress

57. Myleene Klass, singer and model

58. Nannette Klatt, actress

59. Liz Kouri, actress

60. Olga Kurylenko, model and actress

61. Jasmine Lobe actress

62. Emma Loman (alias), German actress

63. Ivana Lowell, author and daughter of Lady Caroline Blackwood

64. Laura Madden, Weinstein employee

65. Madonna, singer-songwriter and actress

66. Natassia Malthe, actress

67. Jessica Mann, former[81] aspiring[82]actress

68. Julianna Margulies, actress

69. Brit Marling, actress

70. Sarah Ann Masse, actress, comedian, and writer

71. Ashley Matthau, actress

72. Rose McGowan, actress

73. Natalie Mendoza, actress

74. Sophie Morris, administrative assistant

75. Katya Mtsitouridze, TV hostess and head of Russian film body Roskino

76. Emily Nestor, Weinstein employee

77. Jennifer Siebel Newsom, documentary filmmaker and actress

78. Connie Nielsen, actress

79. Kadian Noble, actress

80. Lupita Nyong'o, actress

81. Lauren O'Connor, Weinstein employee

82. Gwyneth Paltrow, actress

83. Samantha Panagrosso, former model

84. Zelda Perkins, Weinstein employee

85. Vu Thu Phuong, actress and businesswoman

86. Sarah Polley, actress, writer, and director

87. Emanuela Postacchini, actress

88. Monica Potter, actress

89. Aishwarya Rai, actress

90. Tomi-Ann Roberts, professor of psychology and former aspiring actress

91. Lisa Rose, Miramax employee

92. Erika Rosenbaum, actress

93. Melissa Sagemiller, actress

94. Annabella Sciorra, actress

95. Léa Seydoux, actress

96. Lauren Sivan, journalist

97. Chelsea Skidmore, actress and comedian

98. Mira Sorvino, actress

99. Kaja Sokola, model

100. Tara Subkoff, actress

101. Melissa Thompson

102. Uma Thurman, actress

103. Paula Wachowiak, Weinstein employee

104. Wende Walsh, model and aspiring actress

105. Paula Williams, actress

106. Sean Young, actress

Rape Victims

1. Lysette Anthony told British police in October 2017 that Weinstein raped her in the late 1980s at her home in London.

2. Asia Argento told *The New Yorker* that in 1997, Weinstein invited her into a hotel room, "pulled her skirt up, forced her legs apart, and performed oral sex on her as she repeatedly told him to stop."

3. Wedil David an actress said that in 2016, Harvey Weinstein raped her in a Beverly Hills hotel room.

4. Paz de la Huerta said Weinstein had raped her on two separate occasions in November and December 2010.

5. Lucia Evans said, after a business meeting in 2004, Weinstein forced her to perform oral sex on him.

6. Hope Exiner d'Amore, a former employee of Weinstein, said he raped her during a business trip to New York in the late 1970s.

7. Miriam "Mimi" Haleyi, a production crew member, said Weinstein forcibly performed oral sex on her in his New York City apartment in 2006 when she was in her twenties.

8. Dominique Huett said Weinstein forcibly performed oral sex on her and then carried out another sexual act in front of her.

9. Natassia Malthe said in 2008, Weinstein barged into her London hotel room at night and raped her.

10. Jessica Mann testified in 2020 that Weinstein raped her, on March 18, 2013.

11. Rose McGowan wrote on Twitter that she told the Amazon Studios head Roy Price that Weinstein had raped her, but Price ignored this and continued collaborating with Weinstein. Price later resigned from his post following sexual harassment allegations against him.

12. Annabella Sciorra said, in the early 1990s, Weinstein forced himself into her apartment, shoved her onto her bed and raped her.

13. Melissa Thompson, a tech entrepreneur, told Sky News Weinstein raped her in his hotel room following a business meeting in 2011.

14. Wende Walsh, model and aspiring actress said that when she was working as a waitress at an Elmwood Avenue bar in the late 1970s, Weinstein begged her for a ride and then once inside the car, he sexually assaulted her.

15. An unnamed woman told *The New Yorker* that Weinstein invited her into a hotel room on a pretext, and "forced himself on [her] sexually" despite her protests.

16. An unnamed actress told the *Los Angeles Times* that in 2013, Weinstein "bullied his way" into her hotel room, grabbed her by the hair, dragged her into the bathroom and raped her.

17. An anonymous woman who works in the film industry says in a civil claim she filed in the U.K. in November 2017 that he sexually assaulted her several times sometime after 2000.

18. An unnamed Canadian actress says he sexually assaulted her in 2000. She filed suit against him in 2017.

19. An unnamed actress sued Weinstein for sexual battery and assault, alleging that in 2016 he forced her into sex.

20. An unnamed industry acquaintance sued Weinstein for rape, alleging that he raped her during a 2000 presidential debate.

Source:

https://en.m.wikipedia.org/wiki/Harvey_Weinstein_sexual_abuse_cases#Sexual_harassment_or_assault

2017

一位華人女性的 # MeToo 運動

2017 年 10 月 5 日紐約時報刊登了記者 Jodi Kantor 及 Megan Twohey 調查及追蹤美國著名製片人 Harvey Weinstein 在過去三十年來對女演員及工作人員性騷擾及性侵的故事 - *"How Harvey Weinstein paid off sexual harassment accuser for decades."*

在報導登出來之前，她們互問，「你覺得會有人看嗎？」沒想到她們的報導不但有人看，她們還寫了三篇後續，最後她們得了 2018 年普立茲公共服務獎，出版了一本書「*Breaking the sexual harassment story that helped ignite a movement-- She Said*」。

職場上的性騷擾及性侵，已經到了司空見慣的地步，在亞洲國家裡，男性上司更是有上千年性侵女性下屬的歷史。

1998 年夏天，剛從牛津大學畢業的趙蘊蔚 Rowena Chiu 被 Weinstein 雇為助理，Weinstein 的魔爪很快的就伸向 24 歲的她。當她一個人上班時，她必須不停的阻止 Weinstein 把她頂到床頭，他並裸著身子在房間裡走來走去。她向另外一位秘書 Zelda Perkins 訴苦，並決定辭職，Zelda 不但跟她一起辭職，還向 Weinstein 抗議。Weinstein 的律師很快就出面了，要她們兩人簽保密協議 *Nondisclosure agreement NDA*，並付封口費了事。她們決定把故事告訴媒體，卻發現整個體系都不支持她們，「妳們說的，誰會信呢？」

二十一年之後，在 紐約時報 的文章刊出十天後，女演員 Alyssa Milano 在推特 Twitter 上要求大家響應，"如果妳曾遭到性騷擾，請回覆我 "me too"." 沒想到 #MeToo 運動就在全世界引爆了，臉書在 24 小時內有 4.7 百萬人回應，各國女性都在社群媒體上痛苦的回憶她們被性侵、性騷擾的經驗。這個運動也讓很多有權有勢的男性丟了工作。

　　等了二十一年正義的趙蘊蔚 Rowena Chiu 終於等到了這一天，她說，“我們有責任及義務去揭發像 Weinstein 這類有權有勢的惡棍及他的行徑，唯有這樣，未來的年輕女性在面臨同樣的騷擾時，才會知道這是犯法的，才會知道應該怎麼對付。”

2018

Chanel Miller changed the laws on sexual assault

People v. Turner, No. H043709, 2018
WL 3751731 (Cal. Ct. App. Aug. 8, 2018)

On the night of January 17, 2015, two Stanford graduate students found Chanel Miller lying on the ground behind a dumpster with another Stanford student Brock Turner, on top of her. Miller was unconscious. Turner was arrested and indicted on five sexual assault charges.

In 2016, Turner was convicted of three out of five sexual assault charges against him and sentenced to six months' imprisonment—a sentence which sparked public outrage due to its leniency.

TURNER'S CRIMNE AND PUNISHMENT

In 2015, just two days after his arrest, Stanford announced Turner had been banned from ever setting foot on campus again—the harshest disciplinary sanction it can impose on a student.

On June 10, 2016, the USA National Swimming Team reiterated that Turner would never be welcome in its ranks again, under its zero-tolerance policy for sexual misconduct. That announcement effectively banned Turner from ever participating in a competitive swimming event for the United States.

On August 8, 2018, Turner lost his appeal to overturn his conviction. The California Court of Appeal concluded that Turner must register as a sex offender for the rest of his life.

CALIFORNIA LEGISLATION

The public outrage at the sentence in the Turner case prompted the California State Legislature to pass two bills that changed California state law on sexual assault.

Assembly Bill 701 broaden California's definition of rape to include digital as well as penile penetration. Assembly *Bill 2888* provide for a mandatory minimum three-year prison sentence for sexual assault of an unconscious or intoxicated person.

The final versions of *AB 701* and *AB 2888* were both unanimously approved by the California legislature and were signed into law by Governor Jerry Brown on October 3, 2016.

JUDGE PERSKY RECALLED

Online petitions calling for Judge Persky to be removed attracted over a million signatures by June 10, 2016. Professor Michele Dauber of the Stanford Law School and longtime advocate on the prevention of campus sexual assault, led the *Committee to Recall Judge Persky*. The recall gathering 90,000 verified signatures, and the recall issue was on the state elections ballot on June 5, 2018.

Nearly 200,000 Santa Clara County voters turned out, voting to remove Persky by 61.51%. Persky was the first judge to be recalled in California in eighty-six years, and the first in the United States since 1977.

CHANEL'S VICTIM IMPACT STATEMENT WAS READ INTO CONGRESSIOINAL RECORD

Sexual assault victims can read his or her victim impact statement at the convicted person's sentencing and at any subsequent parole hearings. The right is guaranteed

through the Law Enforcement Act of 1994.

Chanel Millers' 7,247-word-long victim impact statement was published by Buzzfeed the day after Turner was sentenced, and was reprinted in other major news outlets such as the New York Times. It was read 11 million times in four days after it was published, going viral.

On June 15, 2016, a bipartisan group of eighteen members of the House of Representatives took turns reading aloud the statement on the House floor. Representative Jackie Speier organized the reading to raise awareness about sexual assault in general, and to promote her legislation addressing campus sexual assault.

BROCK TURNER BECOMES THE TEXTBOOK DEFINITION OF A RAPIST

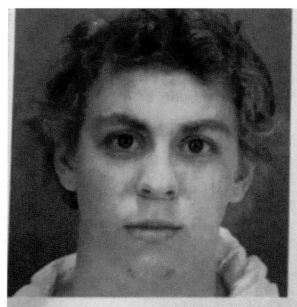

Brock Turner, a Stanford student who raped and assaulted an unconscious female college student behind a dumpster at a fraternity party, was recently released from jail after serving only three months. Some are shocked at how short this sentence is. Others who are more familiar with the

Rape is another example of a crime that has se sion in its definition over time. While rape has al crime and considered *mala in se*, how it has been le has changed. For example, originally, the FBI define "carnal knowledge of a female forcibly and against 2011, the FBI definition was changed to broaden that are considered rape: "penetration, no matter the vagina or anus with a body part or object, or tion by a sex organ of another person, without the victim." This change included boys and men as vic behavior beyond the penetration of a vagina by a the FBI removed the word *forcibly* from this defini reflect contemporary understanding of this viole not necessarily involve force, but it does involve a such as when a person is unconscious. A recent hi example is that of rapist Brock Turner. Turner, a stu University, was caught in the act, and ultimate three felony charges: assault with intent to rape woman, sexually penetrating an intoxicated perso object, and sexually penetrating an unconscious p eign object. Turner's victim was unconscious dur it happened behind a trash container outside of fraternity house on campus.

The second edition of the criminal justice textbook, *Introduction to Criminal Justice* by University of Colorado Professors Callie Marie Rennison and Mary Dodge, uses Turner's mugshot as the accompanying photo in the entry that defines rape.

RISING FROM THE ASHES

In September 2019, Miller relinquished her anonymity and released a book entitled *Know My Name: A Memoir* in which she discusses the assault, trial, and aftermath. The book became a best-seller and was named one of the top ten books of 2019 by The *Washington Post.* The *New York Times* selected the book for its 100 Notable Books of 2019.

In 2016 and 2019, *Glamour* magazine twice named Miller "Woman of the Year" for changing the conversation about sexual assault forever. She was listed as an influential person in *Time's 2019 100 Next List.*

Chanel and father Chris, sister Tiffany, 2016

Mom was proud of Chanel's being selected Time's 2019 100 Next List

2018

浴火鳳凰 張小夏

2015 年的 1 月，張小夏 (她的英文名字叫 Chanel Miller) 去參加史丹福大學的一個晚會，她醉倒了，兩個路過的學生看到她動也不動的躺在不遠的垃圾箱後面，她身上有個男生正在強暴她。強暴犯是史丹福大學的學生、游泳隊明星 Brock Turner。Turner 遭到起訴，檢察官建議六年監禁，但法官 Aaron Persky 卻輕判他六個月徒刑，Turner 只坐了三個月牢就出獄了。

這樣的性侵案件在美國並不罕見，但是願意站出來打官司的人少之又少，一是當事人不願自己的身份和隱私曝光，二是打官司非常勞心傷財。雖然張小夏的案子是地區檢察官主動起訴的，但是她如果輸了這場官司，她就可能永遠生活在性侵的陰暗當中。

張小夏立言

根據 1974 年的 *Law Enforcement Act*，性侵案的被害人可以在性侵者將被法官判決刑期時，朗讀她的" 受害人影響陳述 "。張小夏寫的" 受害人影響陳述 "直指人心，把性侵受害者承受的煎熬、恥辱和憤怒表達的淋漓盡致。這份" 受害人影響陳述 "在法官公佈審判結果後的第二天，被公佈到 *BuzzFeed* 網站，在 4 天內得到 1,100 萬次的點擊。她的陳述開頭是這樣寫的，'You don't know me, but you've been inside me, and that's why we're here today。現在這份" 受害人影響陳述 "已成為紐約四所大學的文學教材，並被美國國會存進重要的歷史文獻檔。

加州立性侵新法

Turner 案件的連鎖效應是加州議會迅速通過兩個法案，更新性侵害相關的州法。*Assembly Bill 701* 擴充對於強暴的定義，現在強暴除了陰莖的侵入外，還包括手指、腳趾及身體其他末梢部位的侵入。Assembly Bill 2888 規定性侵不醒人事或酒醉的人，將遭強制判罪最低三年有期徒刑。*Bill 2888* 及 *Bill 701* 在加州議會全數通過，由州長 Jerry Brown 於 2016 年 9 月 3 日簽字成為法律。

判案法官被罷黜

輕判性侵史丹佛學生的法官引起眾怒，民眾很快的就在史丹佛大學法學教授 Michele Dauber 的帶領下，發起了要求罷黜法官 Persky 的請願。2018 年加州大選公民投票正式罷黜了 Persky，他成為加州 86 年來第一位被罷免的法官，也是美國自 1977 年以來第一位被罷免的法官。

浴火鳳凰張小夏

張小夏的故事席捲西方媒體，The New York Times、CNN、NPR、Yahoo、LA Times、BBC 等都大篇幅報導了她的故事，CBS 電視節目 *60 分鐘* 對她進行了採訪。2019 年，她決定不再隱名埋姓，勇敢的用真名發表新書 ***Know My Name : A Memoir***，該書立刻登上亞馬遜新書排行榜的前幾名。

她在書中寫到，"之前，我一直希望這次的性侵不要成為我生活的一部分，但現在，我已經接受它會一直是我生活的一部分，我只能試著弄清楚它在我的生活中的位置。"

2016 年及 2019 年，*美國時髦雜誌* Glamour 兩度宣佈張小夏為年度風雲女性。2019 年的*時報雜誌*頒獎給她，肯定她是未來 100 位最傑出的人才。張小夏於 2020 年 12 月入選 Forbes「30 位 30 歲以下精英榜」。

張小夏現在恢復了她的本名，和她的名字同時浮出水面的是她的華裔身份。張小夏說，轟轟烈烈的 # MeToo 運動給她站出來的勇氣。之前她一直被認為是白人，但她有一半華裔血統。她的母親張慈說，"張小夏新書的封面有三個金線條，像是日本陶瓷的裂縫是用金子來補的，它的寓意是：萬物皆有裂痕，那就是光進來的地方。"張慈說，"上天選擇了張小夏來經歷這一切，但願她用這名氣為那些遭到性侵的弱者爭取權利。"

2020

Linda Liu Sun is the first elected Chinese American female judge in Los Angeles County Superior Court

Linda Liu Sun was born and raised in Hong Kong. She came to the U.S. for college and graduated from UCLA with a bachelor degree. Her public service work began by serving as Special Assistant to the late Secretary of State, Dr. March Fong Eu until Dr. Eu was appointed as US Ambassador to Micronesia.

In 2001, she was hired as Deputy Attorney General in the licensing section of California Department of Justice specializing in consumer protection litigation.

She had prosecuted 1000 cases involving unscrupulous licensed professionals. In 2015, she was promoted to Supervisor Deputy Attorney General.

In March 3rd, 2020, she was elected as the Superior Court Judge of Los Angeles County.

2020

劉馨儀成為第一位洛杉磯郡高等法院華人女法官

　　出生於香港的劉馨儀，十八歲時隻身到美國唸大學。她的公職生涯從做為加州州務卿余江月桂博士的特別助理開始，一直到余博士成為美國駐密克羅尼西亞聯邦的大使止。

　　2001 年，她成為加州司法部牌照科副檢察長，專司消費者保護的訴訟，起訴了上千個不道德的執牌專業人士。2015 年她被晉升為主管副檢察長。

　　2020 年 3 月 3 日，她當選洛杉磯郡高等法院法官。

Chinese American women elected to lead

美國華人女性躍登政壇

2000

Carol Liu became the first Chinese American state senator

In 2000 and 2003, Carol Liu was elected to the California House of Representatives representing the 44th District in Ventura County. In 2008, she was elected to the State Senate and became the first Chinese American California state senator.

Among her major accomplishments in the senate has been the enactment of Senate Bill 110, *the Crime Victims with Disabilities Act of 2010*. The bill passed unanimously by the legislature and signed into law by Governor Arnold Schwarzenegger, the bill assures that abuse and neglect of people with disabilities and elders are treated as crimes.

2000

劉璿卿是第一位華人州參議員

　　劉璿卿於 2000 年當選加州眾議員，代表第 44 選區，任期兩屆，2008 年，她當選加州參議員，代表第 21 選區至今。她也是加利福尼亞州首位華裔女性參議員。

　　她在州議會的重要政績包括制訂州參議院第 110 號法案—*2010 年殘障犯罪被害人法*，該法由參議院全體無異議通過，並由州長史瓦辛吉簽署成為法律，確認虐待及忽略殘障及年長者為違法。

2006

Ellen Young was the first Chinese American woman elected to the New York State Assembly

Ellen Young was born in Taiwan. She was elected to the New York State Assembly representing the 22nd district for Flushing in 2006.

Young passed five bills into law, including a measure to extend senior citizen services.

In 2008, she lost her re-election to Grace Meng.

2006

楊愛倫是紐約州第一位華人女性州眾議員

楊愛倫，生於臺灣，1977 年移民美國，2006 年當選紐約州眾議員，她是紐約州第一位華人女性州眾議員，也是美國東岸首位當選公職的台灣裔女性。她參與制訂五項法律，包括延長對老人的服務。

2008 年她競選連任失敗，2009 年卸任議員。

2012

Grace Meng became the second Chinese American Congresswoman

Grace Meng is a member of the United States House of Representatives, representing New York's 6th congressional district. Previously in 2006, she served as a member of the New York State Assembly.

She is of Taiwanese descent. Her father Jimmy Meng was elected to the legislature in New York State in 2004 and served one term.

Grace Meng decided to run to succeed her father, but was taken off the ballot when Democrat Ellen Young challenged her residency status. Subsequently, her district residency issues were resolved. Ellen Young succeeded Jimmy Meng in 2006.

In 2008, Grace challenged and defeated the incumbent Young in the Democratic primary. She went on to win the 2008 November election. In 2010, she was re-elected to a second term, unopposed.

She was the author of the *Reverse Mortgage Act of 2009* that prohibited proceeds received from reverse mortgages from being considered as income, so that senior citizens could get their partial property tax exemption.

On November 6, 2012, she became the second Chinese American woman elected to Congress from New York and the first Taiwanese American Congresswoman. In November, 2018, she won re-election with flying colors.

2012

孟昭文成為第二位華裔女性聯邦眾議員

孟昭文生於美國紐約市皇后區，曾任紐約州眾議員，2012 年，她當選美國聯邦眾議員。她是第二位華裔女眾議員（第一位是趙美心），也是第一位台灣裔聯邦女眾議員。

孟昭文的父母都來自臺灣。其父孟廣瑞生於台灣，後移民美國紐約市。孟廣瑞在 2004 年成為紐約州首位亞裔州眾議員，代表第 22 選區。

2008 年 9 月 9 日，他的女兒孟昭文擊敗同選區的楊愛倫，代表美國民主黨，成為紐約州眾議員。

她是 2009 年「*反向抵押貸款法*」的起草人，該法禁止反向抵押貸款之所得被視為收入，所以年長者可以獲得部分房地產稅減免。

2012 年 11 月，她成為美國聯邦眾議員，是第二位華裔聯邦女眾議員。2018 年 11 月，她高票當選連任。

2014

Susan Clair Lee is the first Chinese American woman elected to the Maryland House and State Senate

Susan Clair Lee was elected to the Maryland State Senate in 2014 and 2018. She had previously served in the Maryland House of Delegates since 2002.

She is the first Chinese American woman elected to both the Maryland State House and Senate.

She led efforts to pass an aggressive agenda of laws to fight domestic violence and human trafficking, economically empower women, reduce health care disparities, and obtain funding for rape crisis centers.

Lee has been on the forefront of identity theft, online fraud, consumer protection, cyber security, telemedicine, and bioscience issues. She authored the landmark *Maryland Security Freeze* legislation, the nation's first ever identity theft pre-texting law, introduced and passed Maryland's first *Telemedicine law* creating the *Maryland Commission on Cyber Security Innovation and Excellence,* and other legislation to promote bioscience and emerging technologies.

2014

李鳳遷是第一位馬利蘭州華人女性參議員

李鳳遷律師於 2014 年當選馬利蘭州參議員，2018 年，她獲得 80% 的選票連任。她從 2002 年起即進入政壇，當時她是馬利蘭州的眾議員。

她是第一個美國華人女性被選入馬利蘭州參議會，也是第一個進入馬利蘭州議會的美籍華人。

她在對抗家庭暴力、阻止人口販賣、經濟上賦予婦女權力、減輕醫療保健的貧富差距、注資「*強暴危機處理中心*」的各項立法上，功勳卓著。

她領銜於防止身份竊盜、網路詐欺、消費者保護、網路安全、遠程醫療及生物科學議題上的立法。

她撰寫了馬利蘭州第一個「安全凍結法」，這也是全美國第一個禁止身份竊盜的假託法，在她的努力下，馬利蘭州通過「*遠程醫療法*」，並因此建立「*網路安全創新與卓越委員會*」，促進生物科學及新興科技的立法。

2015

Stephanie Gray Chang is the first Chinese American woman elected to the Michigan State House and Senate

STEPHANIE CHANG
STATE SENATOR

Stephanie Gray Chang's parents were from Taiwan and settled in Canton, Michigan, where she was raised. She said being the daughter of immigrants really shaped her values. She believes in opportunity for everyone, and that is the promise of this country.

Chang first ran for Michigan's House of Representatives of the 6th district in November 2014, knocked on every door in her district twice. She was elected, becoming the first Chinese American woman to serve in the Michigan Legislature. She won re-election in 2016.

In January, 2019, Chang became the first Chinese American Michigan State Senator of the 1st district.

2015

張理成為第一位華裔密西根州眾議員及參議員

　　張理的父母來自台灣，隨後定居密西根州，她說移民父母定義了她的價值觀，她相信父母會來美國，是因為在這個國家裡每個人都有機會。

　　張理於 2015-2018 年擔任兩屆密西根州第六選區的眾議員，表現出色。她在選前敲遍了選區中每間屋子的門兩次，因此她熟知選民關心的議題。

　　2019 年，張理在密西根州第一選區獲得約 75% 的選票支持，當選為該州參議員。

2016

Yuh-Line Niou is the first Chinese American woman representing New York's Chinatown

Yu-Line Niou is a Taiwanese American politician. In November 2016, she won the general election with 76% of the vote to become the first Chinese American New York State Assemblywoman representing the 65th district including Chinatown and the Lower East Side.

Few Chinese American youth were active in politics until Niou's campaign attracted more than 200 student volunteers. Those young volunteers in turn convinced their parents to believe that in order to have a better life, they should be more involved in politics and have their voices heard.

Niou proclaimed, "Let us move forward, one step at a time, opportunities are being created this way." She was re-elected in November 2018.

2016

牛毓琳是紐約市中國城選出的第一位華裔女性州眾議員

牛毓琳出生於台灣，是民主黨員，2016 年 11 月她當選為紐約州第 65 選區眾議員，她的選區包括曼哈頓華埠及下東城，成為紐約州眾議院有史以來第一位代表紐約市中國城的華人女性眾議員。

在紐約參政的華裔年輕人還很少，但這次牛毓琳參選卻吸引了 200 多位學生義工為她助選，他們連帶影響了父母的觀念，了解要追求更好的生活，就應該要有更多人挺身而出，參與政治，為自己的利益發聲。

她說，" 我們要往前站一步，因為機會就是這樣創造出來的。"

2018 年及 2020 年 , 牛毓琳獲選連任。

2016

Theresa Mah is the first Chinese American woman elected to the Illinois House of Representatives

In March 2016, Theresa Mah (D-Chicago) was not expected to win the Assembly 2nd District Democratic primary race against a well-known politician who had a huge demographic advantage. The census numbers showed the 2nd District had an Asian American voting-age population of 23.5%, vastly smaller than the 53% Latino VAP.

She won because the 2nd District of Illinois was purposely drawn to include Chinatown in order to give Asian Americans some influence in the district.

Her Latino opponent reportedly expected Asian Americans to make up about 18% of the district's final turnout. Instead, the final number was closer to 30%.

Asian American voter turnout was typically far lower, relinquishing their population strength. However, Mah's diligence and a strong campaign got people to the polls.

Mah was a senior advisor in former Governor Pat Quinn's administration, and worked to improve diversity and minority representation in the state government. She was instrumental in drafting the first *Asian American Employment Plan*, increasing voter registration of the Chinese American community, advocating for a new Chinatown library and field house and preventing the closure of the Chinatown Post Office. She was re-elected in November 2018, unopposed.

2016

馬靜儀當選伊利諾州首位華裔眾議員

2016 年 3 月，馬靜儀參加伊利諾州第二選區民主黨眾議員初選時，沒人看好她，因為她拉丁裔的對手不但擁有政治世家的加持，而且在該區選民組成中，拉丁裔佔 53%，亞裔只有 23.5%.

馬靜儀後來勝選了，主要是因為伊利諾州將第二選區重劃，將中國城納入，讓該區的亞裔擁有一些影響力，其次是對手預估亞裔的投票率只有 18%，沒想到最後計算出來的投票率將近 30%。

第二選區亞裔的投票率一向比其人口比例低，但這次可不同了，因為他們現在有位合理的候選人可以投給她，而且這位候選人花了很多時間、精力及費用來方便他們投票。

馬靜儀是前州長 Pat Quinn 辦公室的資深顧問，她致力於增加州政府內族群多元化及雇用少數族群，她是*亞裔美國人雇用計畫*的主要起草人，她鼓勵美國華人登記自己的選票，提倡中國城新圖書館及室內運動場的建立，並阻止中國城郵局的關門。

2018 年 11 月，她在沒有對手的選舉中獲選連任。

2016

Lily Mei is the first Chinese American Woman Mayor of Fremont, California

Mayor Lily Mei was sworn in December 2016 as Fremont's first woman and minority Mayor in the city's 63 history. She was first elected to the Fremont City Council in 2014.

Mayor Mei grew up in Philadelphia, Pennsylvania, raised by both parents who immigrated from Taiwan. Lily's professional experience included over 20 years in competitive analysis, product and channel management, supply chain practices, and serving as a worldwide sales operation controller. She ran for Mayor after two years serving in Fremont's City Council.

In July 2019, her plan to address homelessness met serious opposition. Therefore, she asked her residents to practice compassion as Fremont evaluated plans for a *Housing Navigation Center* for the homeless. A *Housing Navigation Center* is a facility designed to provide a clean and safe environment to facilitate homeless persons with the twin goals of rebuilding their lives and focusing on finding stable permanent housing. The first *Navigation Center* was opened in mid-2020.

In June 2020, in the midst of the *Black Lives Matter* movement, more than 300 people demonstrated outside a barricaded police department, demanding change. Mayor Mei faced strong criticism after refusing to kneel with protesters earlier. On June 4, she said, "For myself as a Christian, I do not kneel, except for when I am praying, " Mei said, "And so, therefore, I'd offered-even today-to give an opportunity to get on both my knees and to pray. "

While Mayor Mei received thousands of hate messages during her term, she reiterated her vow to make steadfast progress to benefit Fremont's diverse communities, 50% of whom were was Asian in 2019. In 2020, she won re-election.

2016

高敍加成為加州佛利蒙市第一位華人女市長

高敍加在賓州費城成長，她的父母是來自台灣的移民。她的專業經驗包括 20 年致力於競爭對手分析、產品和行銷管理、供應鏈的執行及操作控管的經驗。她曾做過佛立蒙市議員兩年，於 2016 年被選為市長。

2019 年 7 月，她計劃解決遊民問題時，碰到居民激烈的反對，她要求居民在市政府評估「*住房導航中心*」的計劃時懷惻隱之心。「*住房導航中心*」的目的是提供遊民一個乾淨安全的環境，希望能重建他們的生活，也為他們找到安定的永久住所。佛立蒙第一個「*住房導航中心*」於 2020 年中開放。

在 2020 年 5 月，她考慮到冠狀病毒封城對該市 900 個製造商、210 個供應商、及 10,000 份工作在經濟上的惡劣影響，高市長支持特斯拉的決定重啟製造活動，雖然郡政府繼續對非必要的商業及居民執行「安置到位」，最後大家都同意在進行商業活動時，採取嚴格的安全管理及執行社交距離。

2020 年 6 月，在「黑命珍貴」的運動中，300 多人在警察局前示威，他們要求高市長跟他們一起單膝下跪，以示與黑人團結，高市長拒絕了，她說她只在教堂祈禱時對上帝下跪，但最後在一片混亂中，高市長雙膝下跪，與牧師一起禱告，這是兩全之計，大家都可以各自做出合理的解釋。

2020 年 11 月，她競選連任成功。

2018

Jennifer Gong-Gershowitz is the second Chinese American Woman to serve in the Illinois House of Representatives

Jennifer Gong-Gershowitz is an attorney. She is the granddaughter of Chinese immigrants who were almost deported during the Chinese Exclusion Act period. Their legacy inspired her to pursue human rights and social justice work.

She is the second Chinese American to serve in the Illinois House of Representatives after Theresa Mah (2nd District), representing the 17th district.

2018

江珍妮成為伊利諾州第二位華裔州眾議員

　　江珍妮的祖父母於 1920 年代從廣東台山移民到美國，他們歷經「排華法案」的艱困環境，差點被遞解出境。他們的痛苦讓她持續關注移民權益。在從事多年移民律師工作後，她決定投入伊利諾州 17 選區成為華裔候選人。

　　當選後的江珍妮，會繼續關注人權與社會正義。

2019

Lily Qi is a first-generation Chinese American woman elected to the Maryland House of Delegates

Maryland Assembly woman Lily Qi was born in Shanghai, China. She represents the 15th district in the Maryland House of Delegates since 2019. As a first-generation Chinese American running as a Democrat for a seat in the Maryland state legislature, Qi felt disconnected from the party establishment.

She had worked for years as Montgomery County Executive Isaiah Leggett's chief administrator overseeing economic and workforce development. But Qi lacked the political base and union endorsements, and she knew that immigrants like herself were rarely sought out by politicians in Maryland or elected to office.

Qi turned to the large Asian American immigrant community in her district, writing columns about the U.S. party system in local Chinese-language newspapers and discussing her platform on WeChat, a popular messaging app. She drew hundreds of people to conversations on WeChat.

"Democracy is the best system," Qi said, "But it favors those who participate."

2019

齊麗麗是馬利蘭州的第一代、也是第一位華人女性州眾議員

齊麗麗出生於中國上海，她於2019年當選馬利蘭州眾議員，代表第15選區。作為第一代美國華人，當她以民主黨身份在馬利蘭州競選時，該黨大佬們幾乎沒人跟她聯繫。

雖然她曾在過去幾年擔任蒙哥馬利郡主席 Isaiah Leggett 的行政副長官，主管經濟和勞動力的發展，但齊麗麗缺乏政治基礎及工會的背書，她知道像她這樣的移民不會被馬利蘭州的政治圈看上或是被任命公職。

所以齊麗麗轉向她選區中最大的亞洲移民社區尋求支持，她在當地的中文報紙上寫專欄，向選民解釋美國的黨派制度，並在社群媒體微信上解釋她的理念，她這下子有了數百位粉絲的支持，最後終於如願以償。

齊麗麗說，「民主是最好的制度，但你也要參加才行。」

PHOTO CREDITS

P.76, 77: Honorable Judge Julie M. Tang

P.79, 81: Wikipedia

P.83~84: Wikipedia

P.86, 88, 89: Ohio Chinese American Association

P.91: Rowena Chiu

P.99: May May Miller

P.101: Creator: Gary Reyes, Credit: San Jose Mercury News

      https://www.google.com/amp/s/www.mercurynews.com/2018/01/11/brock-turner-case-campaign-turns-in-100000-signatures-to-put-judges-recall-on-june-ballot/amp/

P.102: Professor Callie Marie Rennison

P.104, 105: May May Miller

P.108: Honorable Linda Liu Sun

P.111: California State Senate Archives

P.113: Wikipedia

P.115: Wikipedia

P.118: Wikipedia

P.121: Wikipedia

P.123: Wikipedia

P.125: Theresa Mah

P.128, 129: Mayor Lily Mei

P.131: Illinois House of Democratic Caucus

      https://ilhousedems.com/project/rep-jennifer-gong-gershowitz/

P.133: Delegate Qi Lily

ACKNOWLEDGEMENTS

The views expressed in this book are mine. However, I could not have completed the work of such magnitude without the help of many people, including those who assisted me in years past with the exhibition of Herstory.

My special gratitude goes to:

Red & Blue Publishing

Henry Shih-Fang Chen

Yi Mei Chen

Hsien Qi-rei

Li Mingguo

Ann Carroll

Doris Tseng

Yi Liang

May May Miller

Maggie Lo

Herman Chan

Lavinia Chan

Helen Liu

Chanel Miller

Honorable Judge Lilian Sing

Honorable Judge Julie Tang

Zoey Weng

Lotus Yee Fong

Delegate Qi Lily

Rowena Chiu

Made in the USA
Monee, IL
11 July 2022

99464632R00083